"*Becoming a Future-Ready Church* is the best comprehensive design book to help leaders fashion the church for the future. For some time, most future-conscious church leaders have known that the church *must* shift its story, scorecard, stewardship, and structure from church-as-institution to church-as-movement (the kingdom expression). Every movement begins with deconstruction—and we've had plenty of that—but now it's time to put some furniture back in the house."

—REGGIE MCNEAL, bestselling author of *The Present Future* and *Kingdom Come*

"If you're tired of the usual doom and gloom about the church's future and looking for fresh voices, research, perspective, and hope for what's next, you'll love this book."

—CAREY NIEUWHOF, author, podcaster, founding pastor, Connexus Church

"*Becoming a Future-Ready Church* challenges us to look beyond treasured modalities by moving past platitudes to take practical steps that ignite hope and inspire action. This book is about leading change. Leading church change is as disruptive as Jesus Christ, who was all about change, jumping the social, political, and religious guard rails of ancient times. He encourages us to do the same even as the tectonic plates of our twenty-first century religious landscape continually shake, rattle, and roll. We need courage to enter this vortex of change. *Becoming a Future-Ready Church* is an invitation to step boldly now!"

—BISHOP VASHTI MURPHY MCKENZIE, president and general secretary, National Council of Churches

"As someone who daily must examine the stark reality of the church's present circumstances while avoiding despair, I thoroughly enjoyed the research-informed yet refreshingly hopeful perspective of *Becoming a Future-Ready Church*. Every religious leader should wrestle with the authors' insights and vision of a Spirit-filled path for the church's future."

—SCOTT THUMMA, PhD, director of the Hartford Institute for Religion Research

"The authors provide a bridge to the future with biblical precedents and current innovative church examples. They unpack the eight crucial shifts that are already happening on the church landscape and offer insightful questions to help church leaders develop *future-ready churches* . . . today. Warning: This book is a game changer!"

—JIM TOMBERLIN, church consultant, coauthor with Warren
Bird of *Better Together: Making Church Mergers Work*

"*Becoming a Future-Ready Church* is a must-read for any leader passionate about equipping the next generation. Daniel Yang, Adelle Banks, and Warren Bird provide a visionary roadmap to navigate the shifting landscape of modern ministry. This book is both a call to action and a practical guide for fostering a vibrant, resilient church community."

—JONATHAN POKLUDA, lead pastor of Harris Creek
Baptist Church, host of *The Becoming Something* podcast,
bestselling author of *Welcoming the Future Church*

"While we can't see into the future, it's wise to study cultural trends and learn from thriving churches. Daniel Yang and Warren Bird, renowned researchers on church growth, along with religion journalist Adelle Banks, share valuable insights in *Becoming a Future-Ready Church*. Their thoughtful approach equips church leaders to innovate prayerfully amidst cultural shifts while staying true to the gospel, ensuring churches continue to impact lives for generations."

—CRAIG GROESCHEL, senior pastor of Life.
Church, author of *Lead Like It Matters*

"If you love the church and have hope for its future, this book is an essential read. Yang, Banks, and Bird's ideas are informed by well-researched analysis and relevant case studies that provide fresh perspectives on how the shifting social structures, culture, and demographics of the United States affect the church. They use these insights, combined with biblically informed missiological thinking, to cast a hopeful and expansive vision for a future church that is more welcoming, restorative, and communal."

—MYAL GREENE, president and CEO, World Relief

"*Becoming a Future-Ready Church* takes a thoughtful look at the challenges churches face in a postmodern, post-Christendom world. It gives leaders both data and permission to dream about new ways of being. Even those who don't share the authors' theology will find stories and practical advice that will stretch their imaginations beyond what they've been taught the church can and should be."

—DAWN ARAUJO-HAWKINS, news editor, *Christian Century*

"Gen Z has to be the most studied generation in human history, and you can get overwhelmed by the nonstop, endless data. Thankfully, the authors concentrate on the underbelly core issues that are repelling the next generation from the church. I'm thankful for their guidance in not just identifying the right problems but giving us direction toward the redemptive alternative that young people long for in church."

—GRANT SKELDON, Next Gen director for THINQ,
author of *The Passion Generation*

"This book is unusual because it not only brims with hope but is also a highly engaging mix of powerful stories and relevant statistics to challenge the status quo. It shows you a series of crossroads ahead, the 'why' behind each issue, and pathways to move forward. But it's not a book to read alone: it's designed for discussion between older and younger leaders. So, let this Scripture-rich guide stimulate your joint conversations about how to proceed!"

—MICHAEL MARTIN, president and CEO, Evangelical
Council for Financial Accountability (ECFA)

"*Becoming a Future-Ready Church* provides vital insights and practical strategies for churches navigating today's rapidly changing landscape. This book is essential reading for church leaders looking to foster deeper engagement, embrace innovation, and thrive with tools they need to navigate complexities. It's a timely resource that empowers churches to adapt and grow while staying true to their mission."

—DAVE FERGUSON, cofounder and president of Exponential,
and CARRIE WILLIAMS, director of ExponentialNext

"The next generation is not the greatest threat to the church but rather the greatest invitation to return to the core values the church was always meant to uphold. This book brilliantly demonstrates that invitation and provides leaders with a practical roadmap for their churches. I highly recommend this volume to every church leader committed to reaching and empowering the next generation."

—HANNAH GRONOWSKI BARNETT, CEO and founder of Generation Distinct, speaker, and author

BECOMING A FUTURE-READY CHURCH

BECOMING A
FUTURE-
READY
CHURCH

8 SHIFTS TO ENCOURAGE
AND EMPOWER THE NEXT
GENERATION OF LEADERS

DANIEL YANG, ADELLE BANKS, AND WARREN BIRD

ZONDERVAN REFLECTIVE

Becoming a Future-Ready Church
Copyright © 2024 by Daniel Yang, Adelle Banks, and Warren Bird

Published in Grand Rapids, Michigan, by Zondervan. Zondervan is a registered trademark of The Zondervan Corporation, L.L.C., a wholly owned subsidiary of HarperCollins Christian Publishing, Inc.

Requests for information should be addressed to customercare@harpercollins.com.

Zondervan titles may be purchased in bulk for educational, business, fundraising, or sales promotional use. For information, please email SpecialMarkets@Zondervan.com.

ISBN 978-0-310-16112-7 (audio)

Library of Congress Cataloging-in-Publication Data

Names: Yang, Daniel, 1979- author. | Banks, Adelle, 1962- author. | Bird, Warren, 1956- author.
Title: Becoming a future-ready church: 8 shifts to encourage and empower the next generation of leaders / Daniel Yang, Adelle Banks, and Warren Bird.
Description: Grand Rapids, Michigan: Zondervan Reflective, [2024] | Includes index.
Identifiers: LCCN 2024013193 (print) | LCCN 2024013194 (ebook) | ISBN 9780310161103 (paperback) | ISBN 9780310161110 (ebook)
Subjects: LCSH: Church renewal. | Christian leadership. | Pastoral theology. | Christianity—Forecasting.
Classification: LCC BV600.3 .Y36 2024 (print) | LCC BV600.3 (ebook) | DDC 262.001/7—dc23/ eng/20240412
LC record available at https://lccn.loc.gov/2024013193
LC ebook record available at https://lccn.loc.gov/2024013194

Cover design and illustration: Faceout Studio, Jeff Miller
Cover imagery: Shutterstock

Printed in the United States of America

24 25 26 27 28 LBC 5 4 3 2 1

From Abraham to Deborah to David to Esther, Scripture inspires us with many stories of people who followed God's leading and took brave and bold actions that would change their own futures. God also used them to change the futures of those who would come after them.

Therefore, we dedicate this book to the innovators in the church and the future generation of innovators after them. May God use this book to help all these innovators connect the unchanging gospel with rising generations who see and experience the world through different eyes.

In the spirit of the psalmist: "Let this be recorded for a generation to come, so that a people yet to be created may praise the Lord" (Psalm 102:18).

Contents

Foreword

It's hard to overstate how much has changed in the world of religion in just the last thirty years. In 1972, only 5 percent of all Americans claimed no religious affiliation. By 2021, that number had risen to 28 percent.[1] Among members of Generation Z, at least 40 percent describe themselves as atheist, agnostic, or nothing in particular ("nones"). However, these shifts are not merely a story about young people leaving religion behind. In 2008, 17 percent of baby boomers reported no religious affiliation; by 2023, the number had risen to 28 percent.[2]

In terms of religious attendance, the numbers are almost hard to fathom. In 2008, about 45 million Americans never attended religious services, while 70 million were attending at least once a week. By 2022, the share of weekly attenders had dropped to 62 million, while the number of never-attenders had jumped to 85 million.[3]

Nearly every major American denomination is smaller today than it was a few decades ago. The United Methodist Church had 11 million members in 1967. Today, that figure is 4.9 million.[4] The number of Southern Baptists had reached its peak in 2006, when the denomination counted 16.2 million on its membership rolls. Now, it is below 13 million for the first time since 1976.[5] The Presbyterian Church (USA)'s membership is down 62 percent since 1987, while the United Church of Christ lost 57 percent of its membership during the same period.[6]

There's no doubt that American Christianity is facing more headwinds than tailwinds. It has never been more difficult to start or grow a church in the United States than right now. How can ministry leaders position their sails to navigate the turbulent waters that are just over the horizon?

While this panorama might seem bleak, there are also some bright spots in American religion. The number of Americans who identify as nondenominational has gone from 3 percent of the country to 15 percent in the last fifty years.[7] Some denominations, such as the Assemblies of God, the Presbyterian Church in America, and the Anglican Church in North America, have boasted positive growth trajectories over the last decade.[8] Even today, while the number of nones is up and church attendance is down, 85 percent of people still believe in God.[9] There is also some emerging evidence that the share of both millennials and Generation Z who identify as atheist, agnostic, or nothing in particular has hit a plateau over the last several years.[10]

Becoming a Future-Ready Church acts as a guide to successfully cross stormy seas. It uses many helpful examples to build the case that the American church has ample reason for hope and that the coming years hold much to be excited about.

This volume is different from other books that address church growth and the future of American religion. It offers the reader a wealth of insights from a number of different perspectives and is woven together with such creativity and care that it should be an indispensable resource for those looking toward the future. Daniel Yang, Adelle Banks, and Warren Bird have come together to form a dream team that offers a gift to pastors and church leaders for years to come.

Daniel is on the cutting edge of evangelism in the United States. Every time I speak with him, I am convinced that he is one of the world's leading experts on how churches can become more welcoming to outsiders while also strengthening their congregational health and vitality.

Adelle brings a wealth of insight into the history and contours of American religion. Her knowledge is hard-won through decades as one of the most dogged and respected reporters on the religion beat.

No one knows the world of religion statistics better than Warren, and his insight comes through in this volume. He pulls together data from a wide variety of sources that would be inaccessible or unavailable to anyone else.

This book is the ideal combination of rigorous statistics and actionable insights for pastors and ministry leaders. I can say this because not only am I a social scientist who studies American religion from a data perspective, but I also have been a bivocational pastor for the last two decades. I work with clergy constantly about challenges facing the church.

Each chapter is organized around a key shift in how churches should approach the future and contains a variety of ways to drive this point home. Of course, there are charts and graphs—which I certainly appreciate—but there are also case studies of churches that are tackling these problems and questionnaires that can be used by congregations to start discussions. By including all these components and keeping its material rooted in a biblical perspective, this book makes it easy for any reader to understand, internalize, strategize, and remain hopeful about the future of the church in the United States.

RYAN P. BURGE, PHD

Founder of *Graphs about Religion* and author of *The Nones: Where They Came From, Who They Are, and Where They Are Going*

Preface

This is a book about hope. As you think about the church's future—and *your* church's future—we want to help you be a thoughtful and sober-minded optimist (1 Peter 1:13). And as we think about the mission and origin of the church, there's much to be hopeful about. After all, Jesus made amazing and all-encompassing claims. He addressed a vast range of human needs and experiences throughout the New Testament gospels, showing how the answers could be found in him and his kingdom to come.

When Jesus's disciples faced heightened anxieties, fears, and troubled hearts (John 14:1), Jesus drew them toward himself, saying, "I am the way, and the truth, and the life" (v. 6). He offered them his "peace" as something far greater than what this world can provide (v. 27). To people feeling the weight of shame and guilt, Jesus offered forgiveness (Mark 2:5; Luke 7:47; 23:43; John 8:11). To those facing injustice, he affirmed, "And will not God bring about justice for his chosen ones, who cry out to him day and night . . . ?" (Luke 18:7 NIV). To those facing death, he said, "I am the resurrection and the life" (John 11:25). And to all who follow him, Jesus declared, "I am come that they may have life, and have it to the full" (John 10:10 NIV).

For each of us authors, Jesus has been all these things and more, especially during the writing of this book. When bad news came from the doctor to one of our households, Scripture's promises brought comfort and hope. During a major job change for another of us, God guided with wisdom and joy. During a season of deep relational pain for yet another of us, God gave new life and renewed purpose.

However, even though church leaders are armed with all this good news—both the promises of God and experiences of God's faithfulness—too many of them are tempted to live like functional atheists, some even wallowing in cynicism. When asked how the churches they serve can become future-ready, many of these leaders pessimistically complain about how stuck things are rather than *declaring* faith in how God wants to work. Too many church narratives are developed out of fear of decline, experiences of disillusion, or feelings of being overworked or overwhelmed. But God rarely uses pessimists to create the future.

We want to tell a better story of how some people are moving from handwringing to hope. For those who have fallen into apathy or despair, we want to inspire dreams of a future for your church that is far better than today. We want to remind you that the best is yet to come, yes, but also that the Best has already come!

This book is written to challenge you, regardless of your church's present condition, to approach the facts of reality with the truth of Scripture so that you can make appropriate and courageous shifts in your ministry model. Not only does your church have hope for a bright future, but we also believe God is calling you, along with the leaders of another generation in your church, to begin shaping that future *today*. Your vision of biblical hope can foster a culture where people will try new things, take creative risks, and employ fresh models to accomplish God's mission.

> While today's churches can indeed help create a better society for that promising future, this will require their leaders to think about how they are setting up the next generation.

While today's churches can indeed help create a better society for that promising future, this will require their leaders to think about how they are setting up the next generation. This applies from the youngest church leader to the oldest (and it is well-established that the U.S. pastorate is aging and many church leaders are waiting longer to retire[1]). Many have speculated about the causes behind a reluctance to hand over the reins to younger leaders, but one thing is clear: ministry leaders are missing a generational handoff. One of our biggest goals in this book is to help your church make that transition by casting a more optimistic vision for the future.

Accordingly, we want readers to move from "What are the best practices for today's models?" to "There's an urgency to discuss the future," and even "Here are possibilities to try." Each chapter tackles a big cultural issue most churches are facing or will soon face and tries to reframe it in a more appealing or approachable way for the next generation.

In short, we wrote *Becoming a Future-Ready Church* to help you prepare your church to innovatively make disciples of Jesus and to work on those plans together as older and younger leaders. This book is a message about encouraging and empowering the next generation of leaders to translate the unchanging gospel for an ever-changing world that thinks—wrongly—that religion is increasingly irrelevant to people's lives.

We start (chapter 1) with the humbling realization that your church is probably using a ministry model that worked best in 1950 to prepare for a culture that is closer to the year 2050. Each of the eight chapters that follow (chapters 2–9) tackles one major shift in how churches should approach their mission. We explore the "why" behind each shift and then suggest practical ways you can prepare your church to thrive as it repositions itself for more effective ministry. We also include a lengthy profile of a specific congregation making the shift as its leaders find new paths to inspire and serve the community both inside and outside the church. Finally, each chapter concludes with action steps for current and rising-generation leaders to discuss together. All along the way, we provide empirical data through significant national research so church leaders have a thoughtful and well-informed trajectory for the future. The conclusion underlines the urgency to begin making changes now and offers further pointers about the next steps to take.

Are church leaders perpetuating institutions and ideas that the next generations are unwilling to maintain? Or will they step up with a hopeful and informed approach that veteran and novice ministry leaders will be eager to embrace together? *Becoming a Future-Ready Church* steers you through eight crucial conversations that will effectively prepare you for the journey ahead.

We modestly pray that this book will guide you in that journey. We ambitiously dream that this endeavor will become a game changer for you and those who lead alongside you.

CHAPTER 1

Why We Need
Future-Ready Churches

"Church as you know it is over. Here's what's next."

No, that's *not* what this book is about. Instead, we coauthors—a missiologist, a religion journalist, and a church researcher—believe that your church's best days could yet be ahead. We invite you to let us guide you as you seek God and search Scripture, even though you are perhaps also feeling out of depth as you wade through the rising waters of today's (and tomorrow's) social and cultural changes. We want to show how you could navigate those waters toward places of health, hope, and growth. As you prepare your church for what's ahead—from organizational course corrections to the rise in mental health issues—we want to equip you for the necessary conversations to move forward in faith and with greater wisdom.

Today's American church is deeply shaped by a particular time in history as well as a culture that no longer exists.

As an essential part of this process, we also want to help you mentor the next generation of leaders needed for the road forward. Frankly, today's American church is deeply shaped by a particular time in history as well as a culture that no longer exists. Thus, one of the most important contributions *Becoming a Future-Ready Church* can make is to help you process the following questions: "Have we built institutions that don't work for the next generation of believers and their leaders? And, if so, what should we do about it?"

Have we built institutions that don't work for the next generation of believers and their leaders?

Consider the church—Akron Baptist Temple—that first met as fourteen people at Rimer Elementary School in Akron, Ohio. In just a few years, it began receiving national recognition for the number of people that were making decisions there to follow Jesus. Over time, it also became an inspiration and training center for hundreds of other churches to do likewise.

The founding pastor of this church, Dallas F. Billington, was a lay-person who had moved from Kentucky to take a factory job in Akron. Significantly, several thousand other people from impoverished areas of Appalachia were doing likewise. Billington, who had become a believer at age twenty-one, obtained an education through remote-learning Bible classes. He was a passionate evangelist with an infectious personality who shared Christ at every opportunity. Besides calling people to follow Jesus at work and in his neighborhood, Billington spoke regularly at a downtown mission, and he started an Akron radio program that billed him as the "Southern Evangelist."

Akron Baptist Temple, which at its peak had a membership of more than ten thousand active participants, was distinctly Southern in its music, preaching, and culture. However, it was also bold, visionary, and downright unstoppable in the ambitious evangelistic activities its leaders would attempt. Several times a year the church sponsored large events to attract community attention, especially in reaching out to children. For example, it held many "Friend Days," encouraging everyone to bring a friend to Sunday school. The church also invited big-name preachers to speak during the year, especially radio personalities whom many had heard but never seen in person.

Elmer Towns, the leading authority on the Sunday school movement, wrote a bestselling book that prominently featured Akron Baptist Temple,[1] and that attracted the attention of the local newspaper. The church subsequently invited Towns to speak at a morning service, where he also presented a plaque recognizing it as the largest Sunday school in America. This was big news, since Beacham Vick's Temple Baptist Church in Detroit, Michigan had previously been generally considered the largest. Local newspapers and television immediately directed a major spotlight on the church.

Beyond local outreach, Akron Baptist Temple developed radio and television programs along with generous missionary support, leading to a worldwide ministry. This congregation became a household name among independent Baptist churches.

As the church expanded, its campus became a jaw-dropper for anyone who visited. Besides the mammoth 263,000-square-foot building (technically, seven interlocking buildings), the property included three sanctuaries (one with 4,000 seats and another with 2,800 seats), a full-size basketball court, two baseball fields, and plenty of parking. The total campus covered twenty-nine acres.

Love it or hate it, everyone in the Akron community knew about this church and about all the cars and buses that flooded there each week. So did thousands of church leaders across the nation.

Looking for a New Future

Wait . . . you haven't heard of Akron Baptist Temple? If not, this might be because the church went into a long decline after its attendance peaked in the 1960s. It ultimately sold its property, moved, and renamed itself. Today, the restarted congregation, chartered in 2019 as Connect Church, meets five miles away in a 375-seat, 20,000-square-foot facility, seeking to reach its new neighborhood for Christ.

Why that name? "We feel that connecting people to Christ, community, and purpose is the most important method to reach people in this day and age," says Jason Knight, the current pastor. He had grown up in Akron Baptist Temple, the third generation in his family to do so, and had been its youth pastor.

Thus, America's largest church in the 1960s no longer exists in location or name. For all the good Akron Baptist Temple did, and for all the godly leaders at the helm there, none were wired to keep the momentum going. The church had initially found a winning leadership formula for outreach, discipleship, and growth, but it couldn't raise up another generation who would thrive at the same level going into the future.

Why? The question of how churches transition over time (or don't!) triggered the writing of this book. Asking "why" questions is imperative, not only so we don't repeat blind spots or failures of the past but also so we create a better context of ministry for the next generation.

> **The question of how churches transition over time (or don't!) triggered the writing of this book.**

Many churches during the 1960s had difficulty trying to navigate the culture around them. Perhaps the Christian bubble was big enough and separate enough from the rest of society that certain questions didn't rise to the forefront. For example, Akron Baptist Temple was largely white. A local newspaper quoted Pastor Billington as simply accepting that fact:

> "Our people are predominantly of Southern heritage," said Billington, referencing Appalachian migrants who settled in Akron around the church. "We have colored folks who come here from time to time, but they usually come once and don't return.
>
> "They just don't seem to feel as welcome here," the church leader said.[2]

Unfortunately, that observation seems to be where the church's investigation into this reality ended. Akron Baptist Temple didn't know how to ask the "why" question underneath African Americans not committing to the church. And while a later pastor affirmed that segregation is "something our church has repented of,"[3] too many churches experience repercussions to this day for not fully addressing their struggles with racial issues in the past—and with other kinds of cultural and biblical issues that construct identity and belonging in the church.

To remedy this situation, this book proposes eight conversations—one per chapter—unpacking the "why" questions underneath complex issues like race, technology, community, and identity that today's churches must discuss. Though we often feel uncomfortable in doing so, asking "why" questions is imperative so we don't repeat failures or maintain blind spots of the past. We can create a better ministry context for the next generation.

Does Every Church Have a Shelf Life?

It's easy to dismiss our question of why Akron Baptist Temple declined by attributing the answer to common understandings of a church's "normal" life cycle. Dallas Billington, born in 1903, moved five hundred miles to Akron in 1925 to work at Goodyear and founded the church nine years later. The church's attendance and impact peaked during its third decade of life (1965–1969). Billington was still pastoring it when he died in 1972 at age sixty-nine. He was followed by his son (1972–1996) and then by his grandson (1996–2007). The next pastor, a nonfamily member, led the church until its eighty-first year (2015), when the congregation of about six hundred voted almost unanimously to put all twenty-nine acres on the market.

The announced reason behind the decision to sell and move involved the question of whether to continue maintaining an aging building or instead to use the church's money and resources to further the gospel mission of reaching and serving others. "Our biggest asset is our biggest liability," the pastor at the time told the local newspaper. "[W]e cannot afford this building and we would not be good stewards of our resources if we did not consider this move."[4]

The congregation relocated to Akron's suburban south, where the majority of its members lived. But, sadly, getting away from the overwhelming facility costs was not enough to create the momentum for a surge of new growth.

Meanwhile, the buyer of the Akron Baptist Temple facilities was a Cleveland-based megachurch that had recently started a campus in Akron. This satellite congregation then moved from its leased facility to the Akron Baptist Temple's larger sanctuary—thus, a predominantly Black church would be continuing the mission of a predominantly white church. This was a very exciting turn of history after Akron Baptist Temple's segregationist roots, but, unfortunately, the purchasing congregation put the property back up for sale a year later. This new campus of the Cleveland megachurch plant had peaked at as many as one thousand attendees, but that number wasn't enough to sustain the upkeep of the immense property, according to the pastor of the Cleveland megachurch.[5]

So, the two churches went their ways—the successor congregation of Akron Baptist Temple having moved five miles south, and the campus of the Cleveland megachurch, now becoming a standalone church, returning to its previous 1,000-seat leased location. Despite the difficult circumstances with the original church facilities, the two pastors remain close friends to this day.

Meanwhile, the Akron Baptist Temple's former property sat idle, the doors covered with plywood. Vandals eventually pried them open. As a local headline summarized the situation two years later, "Once among Biggest U.S. Churches, Empty Akron Baptist Temple Now Home to Looters, Squatters."[6] In mid-2024, the buildings were being demolished.[7]

At the root of church life-cycle questions is the issue of whether a church can continue its first-generation burst of innovation—its creative and sometimes disruptive way of voicing and meeting a genuine need. Too often something changes over time, but church leaders don't catch it. Or they catch it too late. Or they don't know how to respond to it. Or they lack the awareness or courage to have the conversations needed to address the change.

In this book, we will guide you in identifying church practices and ways of thinking from the culture of yesterday that are not enough for today's complex reality. We will also offer suggestions as you seek to find innovations consistent with Scripture that connect with the emerging culture of tomorrow. We strongly affirm that God is the same, yesterday, today, and forever (Heb. 13:8), and likewise that the gospel is the unchanging "once for all" (Jude 3) faith taught and embodied through the Lord Jesus Christ. Our focus is on *other* areas and modern applications where Scripture allows latitude.

The Problem with 1950

Have you ever given serious thought to how much the years around 1950 have shaped your approach to ministry? That is, how closely aligned is your church or ministry with American Christianity in 1950, when it was building toward a heyday? At the time Christianity was America's dominant, growing faith, as Figure 1.1 illustrates. Chances are, you don't think your church's ministry model traces its roots to that era, but we'd like to suggest otherwise.

Figure 1.1—1950s: A Heyday of Sorts for Christians

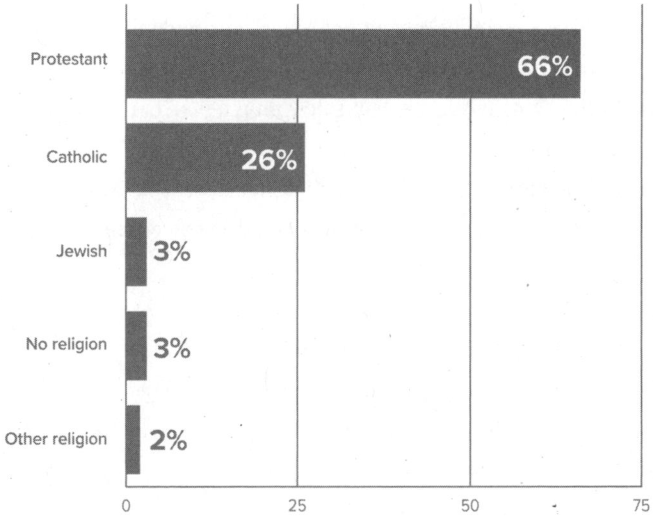

U.S. Census, Current Population Survey, 1957; image courtesy ECFA.

The TV series *Leave It to Beaver* looked at life through the eyes of Theodore "Beaver" Cleaver, eight years old when the series launched in 1957. Each episode showed some aspect of Beaver's growing up with his athletic older brother Wally, a mom who always wore pearls, and a dad who always knew what to do. The show resonated deeply with many viewers since it reflected the best of white, suburban, middle-class America—or at least the family-focused, loving, wholesome approach to life that many idealized and aspired to for that era.

If you could imagine a church designed to reach, serve, and disciple a family like the Cleavers, you might find many churches that would fit this profile *today*. Yet present-day America is far more urban and multiethnic than the world of the Cleavers, with more families fractured and also stressed by mental health challenges. Too many adults, both single and married, are living paycheck to paycheck, among other issues.

Indeed, the American church after World War II did seem to be strong and flourishing: "The period from the late 1940s to the early 1960s was one of exceptional religious observance," wrote one pair of scholars.[8] For example:

- In 1952, a record 75 percent of Americans said religion was "very important" in their lives.[9]
- In 1957, a record 82 percent said that religion "can answer today's problems."[10]
- Nationwide, church membership grew faster than the population, from 57 percent in 1950 to 63 percent in 1960.[11]

Others have noted that by the late 1950s, a record-setting half of all Americans were *attending* church regularly:

The highest historical level of church attendance, about 47% of the U.S. population on an average Sunday, was reached in 1955 and 1958.[12]

Religion flourished, it seemed, in every class, race, region, and denomination, from Catholicism to the African American church. This was also the era when the unprecedentedly successful ministry of Billy Graham was galvanizing a new movement called evangelicalism. Pioneering church planter and apologist Tim Keller observed:

> Mightiest of all was mainline Protestantism, consisting of the Methodist, Lutheran, Episcopal, Presbyterian, American Baptist, and the United Church of Christ (congregational) denominations. Their buildings were at the center of nearly all historic downtowns, their schools and institutions were of the highest prestige and their endowment funds were enormous. And even their theologians, such as Reinhold Niebuhr, were respected public intellectuals, prominently appearing on the cover of *Time* magazine and on network television.[13]

Many denominations, parachurch ministries, and mission organizations likewise took off before and during the 1950s and flourished. Examples of this "golden era" include the founding of Wycliffe Bible Translators (1942), World Relief (1944), Missionary Aviation Fellowship (1945), Every Home for Christ (1946), CRISTA Ministries (1948), Greater Europe Mission (1949), Awana Clubs (1950), Billy Graham Evangelistic Association (1950), World Vision (1950), Cru (1951), Compassion International (1952), Fellowship of Christian Athletes (1954), MAP International (1954), and Christianity Today International (1956).[14]

Yet all that forward momentum soon went into reverse, initially for mainline churches. They went from the late 1950s, when more than 50 percent of adult Americans were part of a mainline church, into years of rapid decline, plummeting to 19 percent in 1988 and 11 percent in 2018.[15] As the late National Council of Churches executive Dean Kelley summarized:

> For the first time in [the] nation's history most of the major church groups stopped growing and began to shrink... Most of these denominations had been growing uninterruptedly since colonial times . . . now they have begun to diminish, reversing a trend of two centuries.[16]

However, today this decline in church involvement is no longer limited to the mainline church. The way the church expresses itself is not working as well as it once did, especially with younger generations. Examples range from the public's loss of confidence in the American church to the rapid rise of the "nones" (people who select "no religious preference" or "nothing in particular" on surveys). These will be explored in later chapters of this book.

> The way the church expresses itself is not working as well as it once did, especially with younger generations.

Economist and futurist Paul Saffo[17] of Stanford University says that if you want to tell the future, you have to look twice as far back into the past. So, as we look back, our take is that the modern practice of church in North America—including even its vision for mission and its approach to leadership—is shaped by post-World War II culture and ministry models that were birthed during the 1950s (and sometimes the 1960s). By understanding this background, readers can gain a better grasp of how our models of church are entrenched in a context of an America that is either quickly fading or perhaps no longer exists.

Our sorting through the data has led to eight research-based, illustration-rich chapters built around ways the church is shifting or needs to shift. Each is aimed at a discussion you should begin now, starting with the "why" behind the changes. In each chapter, we try to help you walk your church "from this . . . to that." We also hope to move your discussions from an outdated question to a better question.

Saul's Armor Still Doesn't Fit

The challenge and complication of how best to prepare your ministry to face the future lies in honoring and not abandoning an older generation while respecting and not overlooking an emerging generation. That is, while it's important to anticipate what's ahead, it's equally essential to process the change of guard needed as a new generation rises into leadership over time.

This dilemma is represented by the Bible's young David. Full of faith, he was eager to fight the battles of his day but was uncomfortable with the armor King Saul gave him (1 Sam. 17:39). Instead, David asked permission to use different tools—an alternative approach that was more about agility and accuracy, and not position and power—to address the challenge of defeating Goliath. Saul agreed, and just as God used David's sling to overcome the giant, so today's ministry leaders will be wise to see the vitality of the future church in America through the eyes of the next generation. These leaders can empower that generation to take more leadership today and bless them to use, in new ways, the diverse ministry approaches anchored in Scripture. The challenges ahead for today's young Davids—the women and men taking over leadership from previous generations—include the change in felt needs among the rising generations, which are shaped heavily by anxiety, skepticism, and fragmentation; the increasing religious disaffiliation of younger generations; and the resultant shrinking percentage of Christians in America. In short, the social narratives shaping Gen Z and younger Americans today are vastly different than the ones from which many churches and church cultural traditions have emerged.

> It's essential to process the change of guard needed as a new generation rises into leadership over time.

> Social narratives shaping younger Americans today are vastly different than the ones from which many churches have emerged.

These trends accentuate the urgency for church leaders—starting now—to evaluate whether the churches they lead are overly entrenched in a culture and society that worked effectively in the past but may not be adapting fast enough for the future.

How Optimistic Are You about Your Church's Future?

You may be fearful or even pessimistic about the future of faith in the United States. Indeed, bad news about church decline dominates the headlines, and much of it is both true and sobering. Many indicators of spiritual vitality are down, prompting painful headlines like "Big Drop in Share of Americans Calling Themselves Christian" in the *New York Times*.[18]

By contrast, *Becoming a Future-Ready Church* offers both hope and optimism rooted in Christ. Regardless of where your church is in its life cycle, we affirm that you have many viable options for the coming days and years. Just to set some context for what's to come in the chapters ahead, did you know that . . . ?

- 100 percent of "dechurched mainstream evangelicals" are actively willing to return to church, and 51 percent of dechurched evangelicals think they will indeed one day return.[19]
- Nearly three in four Americans (71%) are curious about the Bible and/or Jesus, according to a major American Bible Society survey.[20]
- Americans give roughly $500 billion to charity annually, with Christians among the most generous givers, and up to 75 percent of all U.S. charities could be considered religious in nature.[21]
- Financial giving to churches is up, even after the COVID-19 pandemic. One study that compared 2020's median church income to 2023's found that giving saw "a remarkable increase of over 25% since 2020," even after adjusting for inflation.[22]
- The majority of American churches now offer a hybrid of both in-person and online worship services (73% as of 2023), which greatly expands many churches' reach.[23]
- 64 percent of college freshmen attended a religious service frequently or occasionally during the past year.[24]
- 81 percent of Americans say there is something spiritual beyond the natural world.[25]
- While a sobering 80 percent of U.S. adults say that religion's influence in American life is declining (the highest percent in the 22-year history of this ongoing survey), an amazing 57 percent lament the decline and want to see religion's influence grow![26]

- Millennials now form the largest demographic of weekly and monthly church attendees, outpacing Gen Z, Gen X, and boomer attendees.[27]
- Nearly nine in ten churchgoers (89%) agree with the statement "In conversations with my friends, I am proud to say that I am associated with my church." An equally high percentage (88%) agree that "I am generally satisfied with the current leadership of my church."[28] In fact, most churchgoers (84%) are optimistic about the future of their church, as Figure 1.2 illustrates.

Figure 1.2—Most Churchgoers (84%) Optimistic about the Future of Their Church

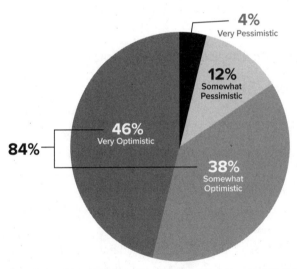

U.S. churchgoers in 2022

4% Very Pessimistic
12% Somewhat Pessimistic
46% Very Optimistic
84%
38% Somewhat Optimistic

Health of Congregations Survey, 2022, Figure 17 (excluding those who "skipped"), Public Religion Research Institute; image courtesy ECFA.

Our Challenge: Implement One-Degree Changes

Each chapter of this book concludes with a section entitled "One Degree of Change."

We've heard stories of ship or airplane captains who miscalculated by just a small amount and ended up far from their destination. When you're traveling somewhere, if you're off course by just one degree, after a mile you'll miss your target by 92.2 feet. On a long journey, that difference will take you to a different city! Suppose you're flying from Seattle, Washington, to Madrid, Spain. If your flight path is off by just one degree, you'll end up instead in the middle of Africa's Sahara Desert!

That one degree of change can also move you in the direction you should have been heading in the first place. If you can genuinely and fundamentally change your church's direction by even a very small percentage, and then stick with your new course, your final destination over time will dramatically change.

Armed with that one-degree idea, our end-of-chapter exercises help you self-assess where you are at present and what conversations you can begin now that can lead to small but significant changes over time.

What's the Research behind This Book?

Business leader Peter Drucker affirmed that humans can't know the future, so he spoke of "the futurity of present events,"[29] indicating that the future is best known by projecting the past. Here are the tools we authors have used in the projections of this book:

- **Prayer:** We paused at the start of our author meetings to ask God for wisdom and guidance. We wanted to be continually sensitive to the promptings of the Holy Spirit.
- **Scripture:** As we identified changing cultural trends, especially the time-locked patterns that emerged in the 1950s, we always sought to root our alternatives in more timeless, biblical foundations.
- **Research:** We have drawn from the best of national research, including groups like Pew Research Center, Gallup, and Faith Communities Today, as well as individual researchers like Ryan Burge and Elizabeth Drescher. Furthermore, we have drawn from

a wide array of writers, from PhD dissertations and consequent publication of these works to news articles across a variety of media.

- **Interviews:** Led by Adelle Banks's award-winning newswriting skills, we have included a fresh in-depth story in each chapter that reveals ground-level insight we might have missed by only focusing on nationwide surveys.
- **Fact-Checking:** This book has gone through a rigorous process of verifying that the facts cited have been accurately reported and carefully proofread.

Scripture is full of warnings about thinking we can predict or control the future. Indeed, we can't determine what happens next. We affirm that only God knows what's ahead and only God controls today, tomorrow, and all of eternity. But we believe the outcome of our painstaking research and writing will give you insights and tools you need to responsibly and proactively use as led by God's Spirit.

Shifting Isn't New

We realize that readers of this book are in different places and situations as they determine what's next for their spiritual family. But perhaps a gentle reminder is in order: Whether you wanted to make changes or not in the past, the time would arrive when shifting was uncomfortable but you did it anyway, often first by initiating courageous conversations. And sometimes the outcome made for a better church, a better staff, and a better you.

"Pivot" was the watchword for many after the COVID-19 pandemic lockdowns went into effect, but before then and since, you may have had to . . .

- accept the retirement (or transfer to another city) of a favorite music minister or Sunday school teacher

- determine that the food at church fellowship time should include healthy options
- learn how to cultivate a compelling digital presence

Hopefully, those changes led to a new musician or teacher with a different outlook that appealed to congregants and children alike, worshippers who were more aware of what they ate, and new attendees who were introduced to your church digitally.

Now, we encourage you to move forward with hope, in the spirit of Jeremiah 29:11: "'For I know the plans I have for you,' declares the LORD, 'plans for welfare and not for evil, to give you a future and a hope.'"

No Better Time than Now

In the year 1900, 82 percent of the world's Christian population lived in the Western world, centered in Europe. Yet by 2000, only 37 percent lived in the West, now dramatically outnumbered by thriving churches in sub-Saharan Africa, South America, and Asia. This shift occurred mostly in just a few decades,[30] and the rest of the world is still catching up to these new realities.

Likewise, tremendous shifts of faith are in motion in North America. Will our churches become like many of the vibrant new churches of the Global South? This could happen. May God use *Becoming a Future-Ready Church* to help you prepare for such a new season ahead. After all, as Figure 1.2 affirms, churches coming out of the pandemic show a remarkable level of optimism about what the future might hold!

Most churches in North America have more in common with 1950 than with 2050. However, even if your model is currently flourishing, your church can't stay where it is if it hopes to be ready for ministry in the future. Your church's best days could well be ahead, even if those days look drastically different from the heydays many of our Christian forebears experienced in the 1950s.

Today is a great day to start preparing your church for an even better future. In fact, there's no better time than *now* to identify what's around the corner and to begin talking about the changes needed to be ready.

This matters because the future is a lot closer than most of us realize. Plus, you need time to navigate appropriate conversations and to develop the next generation necessary for a healthy transition into the future.

If you agree with this outlook, then please say a prayer, turn the page, and get started with the first "from this to that" shift. We open with: How does your idea of church membership and belonging help or hinder how you think about those whom you want to reach? Now invite a leader of a different generation to join you and read it together . . .

CHAPTER 2

From Attendance to Attachment

WHY CHURCH MEMBERSHIP IS LOSING
ITS APPEAL AND WHAT'S REPLACING IT

Dated question: How are we growing church membership and attendance?

Better question: How can we help more people develop healthy spiritual relationships in their complex lives?

THE TREND: Experiencing an increased sense of belonging through new pathways where people explore their identity in Christ with others.

Shift #1: *For most, becoming a church member means exclusively attending and giving to a particular church. But for more recent generations, church membership doesn't always generate feelings of being known and seen. Going forward, church leaders should prioritize not only giving their members a sense of community, but also providing a welcoming space that shapes their sense of identity and belonging.*

One of us authors has a friend we'll call "Maurice." At some point after college, in his mid-twenties—he's not exactly sure when—Maurice realized that he no longer considers himself a "believer"—at least not in the same sense many Christians use the term. As a college student, his personal faith had seemed finally to mature beyond what he had inherited from his mom, the primary person who had raised him. She had been extremely devoted to church for a time after divorcing his dad. While at university, Maurice had gotten involved in campus ministry and was finally able to articulate why he believed certain things about God and the Bible. He attributed much of that newfound confidence in his faith to a yearlong mentoring relationship with a campus Bible study group leader during his sophomore year. Maurice's mentor met with him almost once a week to read the Bible and consume books and podcasts from influential Christian pastors and speakers.

Although the vast majority of Maurice's friends at university weren't Christians or even religious, his campus Bible study group kept him motivated to behave in the ways he believed were consistent with Christian ethics and morality. These included regular church attendance, volunteering in various ministries, personal Bible reading, and drinking only moderately.

For these years as a university student, Maurice belonged to a group of people that affirmed his worldview and kept him accountable for his Christian faith. It was hard for him to imagine making it through college without Christian community. It kept him mentally, emotionally, and spiritually grounded.

After graduation, Maurice found a job and apartment in a town about 30 minutes from campus. Life got busier but simultaneously more boring. So he went out more to treat himself, especially on the weekends. Still, Maurice felt there wasn't much happening that was significant either in his career or social life. His friendships became thinner and less consistent as people continuously moved in and out of his circle. By the age of twenty-eight he was six years into his career, and it had been nearly six years since he last regularly attended church.

20

Figure 2.1—"Not Fitting In"—Top Reason for Not Attending Church

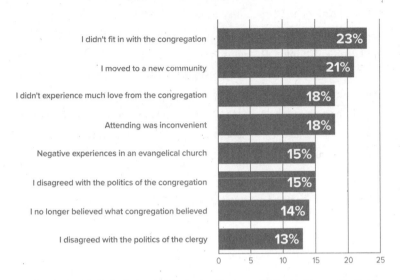

Reason	Percentage
I didn't fit in with the congregation	23%
I moved to a new community	21%
I didn't experience much love from the congregation	18%
Attending was inconvenient	18%
Negative experiences in an evangelical church	15%
I disagreed with the politics of the congregation	15%
I no longer believed what congregation believed	14%
I disagreed with the politics of the clergy	13%

The Great Dechurching by Jim Davis and Michael Graham (Zondervan, 2023, Table 5.1, page 75) with data collection and analysis by Paul Djupe and Ryan Burge; image courtesy ECFA.

When Maurice first moved into his apartment, he had tried going back to the church he attended while in college, but his friends had all graduated and moved away. Now he felt out of place at a church that mainly targeted college students.

Next, Maurice spent some time attending a larger church near his apartment, which was similar to the one he grew up in with his mom. But the church's programming and messaging felt overly geared toward marriage, parenting, and social issues—which did not appeal to him. Plus, Maurice didn't develop any good friends there. Eventually, he stopped attending church altogether.

For a while, Maurice had tremendous cognitive dissonance from his previous high-level commitment to church. A part of him wanted to get back to the naive but zealous person he had been in college. But through a therapist and conversations with coworkers—who experienced a similar journey and no longer consider themselves Christian—Maurice eventually let go of feeling guilty for not being in Christian community. Given all that was happening around him socially, culturally, and in the world of American Christianity, he no longer felt ashamed for not being a good church member. In fact, he was starting to feel a little bit of shame for ever identifying with a church.

At the start of the COVID-19 pandemic, Maurice was asked to take a community health survey given by a local healthcare provider. The survey asked if participants belonged to a church or religious congregation. Maurice checked "no." It also asked about religious affiliation. Maurice debated for about 10 seconds before checking the "nothing in particular" box.

The Undeniable Decline of Church Membership

Most church leaders have strongly valued formal church membership because they take seriously the biblical prescription to "shepherd the flock of God" (1 Peter 5:2). And while there are logistical reasons for why church membership is useful, such as voting, church operations, and programming, the primary reason for why membership still matters today is the tender care and spiritual oversight of people. However, understanding the rapid decline of church membership in America doesn't just tell the story of the rise of secularism in America. The decline of church membership also provides an urgency for church leaders to revisit what they mean by "membership" in the twenty-first century.

> The decline of church membership also provides an urgency for church leaders to revisit what they mean by "membership."

At the start of this decade, two national research projects caught the attention of church leaders across America. The first dataset was from Gallup, entitled *U.S. Church Membership Falls below Majority for First Time*.

In 1937, Gallup began measuring U.S. church membership, initially discovering that 73 percent of Americans belonged to a religious congregation. But that percentage inched downward over the years, and by 2020 the percentage had dropped to 47 percent, as illustrated in Figure 2.2. Gallup suggested that the decline in church membership can be seen by

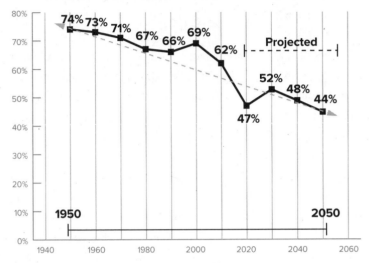

Figure 2.2—Church Membership: Long, Gradual Decline

Question: "Do you happen to be a member of a church, synagogue, or mosque?" (Percentage "yes," with the vast majority responding about church)

Annual Gallup survey from 1938 to present; image courtesy ECFA.

the increase of 1) those who lack religious affiliation and 2) those who do have a religious affiliation but do not belong to a church.[1]

The second study was a data model from the Pew Research Center that perhaps piqued the interest of church leaders even more by providing four future scenarios for the percentage of Christians in the U.S. by 2070:[2]

- **Christianity biggest, but no longer the majority.** In scenario 1, marked by "steady switching," Christians would lose their majority but would still be the largest U.S. religious group in 2070.
- **Christianity eclipsed by the "nones."** In scenario 2, called "rising disaffiliation with limits," "nones" would be the largest group in 2070 but not a majority.

- **Christianity replaced as a majority by the "nones."** In scenario 3, marked by "rising disaffiliation without limits," "nones" would form a slim majority in 2070.
- **Christianity still the majority.** Only in scenario 4, marked by "no switching," would Christians retain their majority through 2070.

None of Pew's scenarios predicted that the percentage of Christians would grow as we approach 2070; these predictions were simply variations of how fast the percentage of Christians would decline in America. Other long-term studies, such as those highlighted by Mark Chaves in *American Religion*, affirm the same news: that every major indicator of American religiosity has declined over recent decades.[3]

Additionally, Gen Z's religious disaffiliation (33%) has outpaced millennials (31%). And this could very well be a part of the larger trend of younger people's distrust of American institutions. According to Gallup, Gen Z's distrust in the U.S. Supreme Court (38%), the presidency (46%), and Congress (50%)[4] seem to mirror its skepticism for hopes in organizations and institutions (such as churches) to bring about societal change.

To many church leaders these datasets are alarming, because they capture a historic and unprecedented magnitude of stories belonging to people similar to Maurice. The reality behind these percentages is that hundreds of thousands, and perhaps even millions of people, have much more complicated spiritual journeys than Maurice's, which represents only one segment of the young adults who no longer consider themselves believers or church members. In short, simply knowing these numbers is not enough for us to understand what's happening underneath them.

Family, Friends, Food . . . and Fido

In *Choosing Our Religion: The Spiritual Lives of America's Nones* (2016),[5] Elizabeth Drescher presented one of the first quantitative and qualitative studies describing the complexity and diversity of nones. Drescher's research helps us see that nones aren't a monolithic group, debunking the notion some have that most nones are highly individualistic atheists and agnostics who reject religion, morality, and ethics.

Drescher categorizes the meaning of spirituality for nones in her study around four things: family, friends, food, and pets or animals (what she refers to as "Fido"). For every person interviewed, at least two of the four categories were mentioned. Nearly two-thirds (63%) of all persons hit on all four categories during the interviews, with only a small group (11%) leaving pets or other animals out of their spiritual narratives.[6]

Drescher isn't saying that nones lack spiritual activities typical for religious groups, such as prayer, Scripture study, or attending worship services or gatherings. Instead, she observes that spiritual practices and belonging look different for nones, especially in their motivation for ethics and social responsibility. This is an important insight, because it demonstrates that nones are capable of experiencing spiritual practices and belonging *without* an ecclesial-like gathering.

> Nones are capable of experiencing spiritual practices and belonging *without* an ecclesial-like gathering.

Many of those Drescher interviewed came from families and friendship circles with strong religious affiliations. After leaving organized religion, some nones struggled to define and maintain these relationships in new ways that didn't center on a common spiritual practice. Moreover, many nones saw these relationships as formative to their spiritual life apart from church attendance and still desired connection to their former spiritual communities. In these cases, spiritual belonging and interactivity with others are much more fluid and integrated with everyday life, events, and networks of relationships. An example of this would be intimacy or an attunement with things like animals or nature.[7]

The Great Swath of the Nones

Given this basic summary of Drescher's findings, it's tempting to think that a large number of people disaffiliated or disinterested in church membership are upper middle class, replacing Sunday worship services with weekly socialite dinner parties. But according to Ryan Burge's *The Nones: Where They Came From, Who They Are, and Where They Are Going*, nothing could be further from the truth. Burge unpacks the profile of those who consider themselves "nothing in particular," which is a categorization of nones found on surveys that track a person's particular religion. He writes:

> Nothing in particulars are the largest group and share little in common with atheists or agnostics. While their gender distribution reflects that of the United States as a whole, they have incredibly low levels of educational attainment, and many of them make below-average incomes. Socially and politically, they are isolated. They don't attend rallies, they don't go to political meetings, and they don't put up political yard signs. . . . However, nothing in particulars represent the fastest-growing religious group in the United States today. Their numbers have increased a full five percentage points in just this past decade.[8]

To continue our opening story, Maurice's younger sister Elizabeth didn't go to college. Although they grew up together living with their mom, Elizabeth didn't have the same academic ambition as Maurice and instead decided to apply for an accounting apprenticeship program after high school. While Maurice moved away for college, Elizabeth stayed home with her mom, attending church with her almost every weekend and even playing the keyboard for its Sunday morning worship band. But when Elizabeth graduated from high school two years after Maurice, she also graduated from her church youth group and inadvertently felt like she had graduated from church altogether. She eventually moved in with her boyfriend, Keith.

By the time the COVID-19 pandemic left America in full lockdown, Elizabeth had already stopped attending any kind of church gathering. And although she had strong feelings about the social unrest across America and the way the government was handling the pandemic, Elizabeth steered clear of any political slogan or position on social media. From what she heard from her mom and former church youth group friends, she grew even more skeptical of the political alignments her former church members were making—many of which she viewed as *mis*alignments. This just further confirmed her sense that the church wasn't any better than the government when it came to social issues.

On occasion, Elizabeth would listen to sermons Maurice sent her from college by either the bestselling author and longtime New York pastor Tim Keller or by the pastor of the church Maurice attended. However, these sermons mostly bored Elizabeth. She was much more interested in the podcasts recommended to her by her girlfriends. Whether at work, in the gym, or driving, Elizabeth was listening to episodes featuring topics like wellness, careers, or relationships. They seemed much more worth her time than speeches by politicians or sermons by pastors.

It's hard to tell if Elizabeth's disenchantment with the church was caused or confirmed by the events of the pandemic, but according to Burge's analysis of decades-long data tracking religious belonging, people like Elizabeth would likely belong to the large swath of people who would identify as "nothing in particular." While both Maurice and Elizabeth would fall into this category, there are more "Elizabeths" than "Maurices" in America, and church attendance now seems silly to both groups.

However, churches that understand human belonging precedes, and perhaps supersedes, organizational membership are able to imagine pathways for people to enter into church life not as religious consumers but as future contributors. That has been the experience of Life.Church.

Life.Church

AMERICA'S LARGEST-ATTENDANCE CHURCH DOESN'T HAVE "MEMBERSHIP"

When Life.Church started in Edmond, Oklahoma, in 1996,[9] it began with a handful of people who, like many congregations, were known as "members."

"In the beginning, membership was a big deal because, as part of a denomination, that's the way everybody was thinking," said Kevin Penry, who was part of the early leadership team of the church, which is affiliated with the Evangelical Covenant Church.

During its first decade, Life.Church had a tradition of asking members to commit annually to a covenant that indicated they would attend, give, and serve the congregation and participate in a small group.

However, on a Commitment Sunday in the mid-2000s, Craig Groeschel, the church's senior pastor, did something unusual: he invited about five other local churches to set up tables in the lobby so attendees, who might be questioning whether or not Life.Church was the right fit for them, could learn about and consider other churches.

"It created this environment of we weren't trying to hang on to people and they felt that freedom, and so they were able to evaluate truly: Okay, is this where I'm supposed to be?" said Penry, 70, who was on Life.Church's leadership team for seventeen years before his retirement in 2017, and is a church consultant today.

Thankfully, few left, Penry added, and the church continued to grow.

As Life.Church became a multisite congregation, its leaders decided to take a different ministry approach that moved away from traditional "membership." Pastor and innovation leader Bobby Gruenewald, 48, who joined the Life.Church staff in 2001, remembers sensing a shift in culture that was a catalyst for the change:

While our mission to reach people for Christ never changes, our ministry methods will continue to change because we're focused on effectively reaching people in today's culture. We're intentional about staying flexible, so if we saw growing trends around the concept of membership, we wouldn't rule it out. But today we're focused on encouraging people to take the next step in their faith journey, which might mean serving, giving, or finding community. For us, the key is to meet people where they are, and help them find the best next step in becoming a fully devoted follower of Christ.

The shift away from membership didn't equate to lower expectations for community involvement; Life.Church has always set a high bar that encourages attenders to be fully engaged. One of their values states, "We are spiritual contributors, not spiritual consumers. The church does not exist for us. We are the church, and we exist for the world." By emphasizing this value, according to Gruenewald, the church seemed to encourage attenders into deeper connection and commitment even as it deemphasized traditional notions of membership. "Being all-in contributors is part of who we are as a church. We lead with a mindset that all of us are called to make a difference in our church and in our communities," he said.

As they encourage individual attenders to focus on others—especially non-Christians—Life.Church's leaders have led the way in putting this advice into action. Its local pastors introduce themselves each week and first-timers are told not to worry about putting a donation in the offering bucket.

"Everything was just immersed in an assumption that we are here interacting with people that have never been here before, who do not know Jesus, and are hurting and looking for a place to belong," Penry said.

This sense of belonging carries into Groeschel's sermons. He uses everyday language that's easily understood by people who don't have any context about church, the Bible, or God. He also considers how his messages might be received by the church's global audience. This might mean acknowledging a physical Life.Church location in New York, Florida, or Kansas, asking members of the Life.Church Online community to type their sermon responses in the chat, or providing extra context around personal stories for someone who may be attending from another country.

"That sent a signal of awareness to the audience: 'Oh, Craig remembers us, he's talking to us. We're not just watching him talk to somebody else,'" added Penry. This focus on individuals to help them see their part in the body of Christ, he continued, often encourages people to make that transition from consumer to contributor.

According to Penry, such a focus—engagement that helps others through service, through giving, or through evangelism—is really the bottom line, semantics aside, for churches of any size and for his colleagues in church leadership. "Engagement is the desired outcome of the terminology of membership," Penry commented regarding Life.Church's hope for the people that show up for weekend services and other activities. "So why not cut straight to what it is that we're looking for? We want you to be engaged in the church."

From Membership and Attendance to Belonging and Identity

We aren't suggesting that churches jettison the concept of membership as they prepare for the future. We also aren't recommending that churches lower their standards for church membership. As you may sense from Life.Church, church leaders can still call people up to a higher standard. Instead, we are suggesting that leaders take time to think deeply and consider how, in the twenty-first century, people have subtly changed the way they think of their own religious affiliation beyond just church membership and attendance. In short, we see the future of church membership becoming more about spaces of belonging and identity formation and less about a list of activities and religious commitments.

> We see the future of church membership becoming more about spaces of belonging and identity formation and less about a list of activities and religious commitments.

For a long time, the strength of someone's religious affiliation in America was pragmatically driven and measured mainly by membership and attendance. Members made donations, voiced opinions, formed a separate category in denominational reports, voted on matters like church budgets and church leadership, and received special benefits to which nonmembers might not have access.

Their attendance usually indicated whether they were an active member in good standing and if they could be relied on to volunteer or to lead a committee. Frequency of attendance has also been a large factor in the way church leaders determined how involved members would be in the life of the church.

To most American adults today, especially boomers and Gen Xers, the following questions make sense: "Which church do you attend?" "Does your church belong to a particular tradition or denomination?" "Do you enjoy being a member at your church?" Here is a possible range of answers:

- "I attend [name of church], and it's part of the [name of tradition]."
- "I attend [name of church], but it's not formally a part of any tradition."
- "I've been church shopping and have been visiting [name(s) of church(es)]."
- "I'm a Christian, but I don't regularly attend church."
- "I'm not a Christian, and I don't attend a church."
- "I don't identify as Christian, but I have been attending [name of church]."

Of course, there are many more variations of these questions and responses. However, why and how they are raised assumes a lot about the way American Christians primarily understood religious affiliation in the twentieth century. These kinds of questions are akin to asking someone about a membership *subscription*: "Are you a Sam's Club or Costco member?" or "Which location do you shop at?" Historically, we've seen religious affiliation in terms of subscription, proximity, and access to goods and services.

> Historically, we've seen religious affiliation in terms of subscription, proximity, and access to goods and services.

In our current century, religious affiliation has become slightly more nuanced, or even more complicated, due to the rise of secularism, individualism, religious pluralism, and nondenominationalism. These trends are leading to the largest number of youth in American history that come from households that are not members of any particular church or perhaps even any particular faith tradition. Moreover, it is not uncommon today—and for the past few decades—for a teenager to have one parent who is Christian and the other parent who is of some other religion or no religion.[10] This teen might attend a youth program at one church during midweek and then a service at a different church on Sunday—or none at all. These family dynamics are continuing to increase and become more complex as society evolves and years go by.

For the last few decades, the growing cultural diversity and changing dynamics of American families have been challenging the boundaries set by traditional church membership and attendance. (We will address this issue more in chapter 3.) Rather than being the primary indicators of a thriving church, concepts of membership and attendance are now more appropriately seen as lagging indicators, giving way to more qualitative approaches for understanding what a meaningful church experience might be like for someone. At their best, parochial models for church membership and attendance can help keep church leaders accountable for the care and service the church can offer to members. But these leaders cannot gauge with precision whether church members have a genuine sense of belonging. This dilemma is true for churches of any size, but it has become especially apparent as we consider millennials and Gen Z.

> Rather than being the primary indicators of a thriving church, membership and attendance are now seen as lagging indicators.

This reality cannot be ignored: millennials and Gen Z have lower rates of church membership and attendance compared to previous generations because they either feel less restricted by society to find belonging and identity in the church or because those needs are met elsewhere. According to Springtide Research Institute's *The State of Religion & Young People 2022* report, 34 percent of young people never attend a religious service and almost just as many (32%) never pray. And the numbers of those who practice yoga or martial arts as a part of their weekly spiritual practice (20%) are slightly more than those who weekly attend a religious service (19%).[11] If there is no social pressure and no perceived benefit to have one's belonging and identity in a religious community, then it makes sense that ideas of church membership and worship attendance have little significance to young people.

Springtide's report also seems to suggest that young people more strongly connect mental health with spirituality than previous generations. That isn't to say that the church and society at large aren't making these connections—the collective awareness for mental health is certainly on the rise. However, mental health—whether in therapeutic or nontherapeutic spaces—is how young people have come to understand vulnerability and safety. For many of them, spiritual spaces and safe spaces are one and the same. Therefore, their idea of belonging—perhaps more so than previous generations—is strongly connected to feeling safe in places sensitive to mental health issues.

Of course, the solution isn't to create arbitrary social pressure or a consumer culture in the church catered toward youth. In particular, shaming a generation for being less religious is a surefire way to create *greater* disaffiliation and perhaps even hostility toward the church. Regardless of how someone feels about church membership and attendance, the human need to belong[12] and our search for spiritual identity will always remain.

> Shaming a generation for being less religious is a surefire way to create *greater* disaffiliation and hostility toward the church.

At our particular time in American Christian history, churches would be negligent if they tried to address membership and attendance without thinking deeply about how they have or haven't provided transparent spaces for people to negotiate (and renegotiate) religious belonging and to explore their own identity formation. For many converging reasons, some millennials and Gen Z never perceive that the church would be a place for discovering these things for themselves. Ignorance or PR issues may very well be keeping these two groups from asking if the church is relevant enough to help them explore these issues. But the church is responsible to be ready and able to say, "Yes, we are relevant, because we are listening!"

These kinds of churches may have to start with leaders asking themselves questions like:

- Why do people isolate and withdraw?
- What spaces are we providing that lift the shame some people are carrying because they are no longer going to a church?
- How can we destigmatize church attendance?
- What are we doing knowingly and unknowingly to create uncomfortable insider–outsider dynamics?

Other follow-up conversations might include:

- How can we as a church teach the broader community about what it means to have healthy social connections?
- How do we as a church provide spaces for people to explore some of their social identities—racial, ethnic, sexual, and especially spiritual identities—with safety and advocacy?

If churches continue to define themselves primarily by who is in and who is out, in terms of membership, they will have difficulty asking these questions with genuine curiosity and bravery. They will also find it difficult to follow where the answers may take them.

> What are we doing knowingly and unknowingly to create uncomfortable insider–outsider dynamics?

Can churches that are looking to the future begin helping people find a new level of belonging and engagement in church today? If churches speak meaningfully to people who are shaped by a culture of casually belonging to organizations, and can help them understand a meaningful sense of belonging and how to achieve it in the various places of their lives—whether or not it is inside the church—then they will be laying down indelible tracks for future church leaders.

One Degree of Change 4

As chapter 1 explained, if you can genuinely and fundamentally change your church's direction by as little as one percent and then stick with this new course, your trajectory will lead to a dramatically different destination. In this chapter, we have called for a shift in posture about the idea of membership. Leaders must start conversations to understand the "why?" behind the changes happening and to frame what churches should do differently going forward. This is especially pertinent as the church you serve speaks to rising generations—which should already be entering into leadership in your church.

Next are simple statements adapted from various ideas presented in this chapter. Use the scale below each statement to assess how much you agree with it, choosing one answer for each row. Then begin some leadership conversations by comparing how much your responses align with the outlook of others in your church. There is space at the bottom of each list item for you to jot down any thoughts or ideas.

1. The idea of "church membership" is losing its appeal, especially among younger generations at our church.

☐	☐	☐	☐	☐
STRONGLY DISAGREE	DISAGREE	UNCERTAIN OR NO OPINION	AGREE	STRONGLY AGREE

2. Someone being a church member today doesn't adequately tell us whether this person has a genuine sense of belonging.

☐ STRONGLY DISAGREE ☐ DISAGREE ☐ UNCERTAIN OR NO OPINION ☐ AGREE ☐ STRONGLY AGREE

3. Our church lacks a good way to measure whether someone has developed a meaningful sense of belonging (i.e., what people need to feel if they have meaningful belonging).

☐ STRONGLY DISAGREE ☐ DISAGREE ☐ UNCERTAIN OR NO OPINION ☐ AGREE ☐ STRONGLY AGREE

4. Our membership process results in people having a strong feeling that "I belong here."

☐ STRONGLY DISAGREE ☐ DISAGREE ☐ UNCERTAIN OR NO OPINION ☐ AGREE ☐ STRONGLY AGREE

5. Too many of our members view their membership as more about their rights and privileges than about what they're becoming through being part of a community.

☐ STRONGLY DISAGREE ☐ DISAGREE ☐ UNCERTAIN OR NO OPINION ☐ AGREE ☐ STRONGLY AGREE

6. As leaders, we've talked about how to frame or reimagine the idea of membership specifically for younger millennials and Gen Zers.

☐   ☐   ☐   ☐   ☐

STRONGLY DISAGREE   DISAGREE   UNCERTAIN OR NO OPINION   AGREE   STRONGLY AGREE

7. Our church needs to tell a better "story" about what church membership means.

☐   ☐   ☐   ☐   ☐

STRONGLY DISAGREE   DISAGREE   UNCERTAIN OR NO OPINION   AGREE   STRONGLY AGREE

CHAPTER 3

From Nuclear Families
to Forged Families

WHY CHURCHES NEED TO SERVE A WIDER RANGE OF HOUSEHOLDS

Dated question: How can we get more people to volunteer so that we can strengthen ministry to the families in our church?
Better question: How can our church's family ministries build health and increased capacity in people so that they can be more available to those who are lonely, struggling, or feeling that they don't fit in?

THE TREND: Promoting family not by limiting ministry expectations to a particular ideal but by facilitating people in various stages of life to connect in Christ-centered community.

Shift #2: *In the past, most churches poured energy into children's ministry but offered little emphasis on marriage or parenting. Currently many churches are also working to champion marriage and family life, but they do far less to support people in other life situations. Going forward, churches will need to find ways* *to welcome and support single adults, single parents, childless couples, and those in other circumstances—from interracial families to those with adopted or foster children to those whose children have mental health challenges.*

For the last several generations, many Christian leaders built ministry around an aspirational vision for the American household. This vision focused on a family composed of a married husband and wife in early middle age—where the husband has a steady career and the wife is mostly home-oriented—raising a few biological children close in age and living in a single-family home in a middle-class neighborhood.

In pop culture, this type of vision has persisted in family sitcoms over the decades in varying degrees:

- *Leave It to Beaver* (1957–1963)
- *Bewitched* (1964–1972)
- *The Jeffersons* (1975–1985)
- *The Cosby Show* (1984–1992)
- *The Fresh Prince of Bel-Air* (1990–1996)
- *George Lopez* (2002–2007)
- *Fresh Off the Boat* (2015–2020)
- *The Upshaws* (2021–present)

Whether or not this vision is what you believe, have experienced, or desire for yourself, some version of it has been seared into the psyche of American culture. Since at least the mid-twentieth century, this model for the American household has played a part in shaping many of our institutions and social structures as they try to embody the value that *"the family* is the building block of society." It has been reflected in the development of city planning, government, education, work-labor division, and, of course, our civic and religious life.

While there are certainly biological factors that form this vision—and, for Christians, biblical factors as well—the socioeconomic development of America as the nation came out of World War II seeking a secure life[1] indelibly shaped the notion of the American household. Roberta L. Coles, emeritus professor of sociology at Marquette University, whose research specializes on the American family, sees its development over three distinct eras: the Agricultural Era (colonial period, 1500 to 1800), the Industrial Era (about 1800 to 1970), and the Service Era (since the 1970s). Coles attributes the 1950s idealism for the development of the American household to the unprecedented economic progress the country was experiencing at the time:

> World War II followed the Great Depression and was accompanied by an economic boom not seen before or since. Also, various government subsidies followed the war and shaped family trends for a period of time. The GI Bill enabled more men to attend college, thus widening the educational gap between men and women. New Federal Housing Administration subsidies and highway construction funds resulted in an explosion of jobs and inexpensive suburban housing, which in turn facilitated "White flight" to the "burbs." The flourishing economy and the people's felt need to make up for time lost during the Depression and war facilitated historic spikes in early and more marriage and childbearing. Hence, the baby boomers, those born between 1946 and 1964, were largely a result of the postwar economic boom, and now, between the ages of 50 and 70, they account for about a quarter of the American population....
>
> Although the lower divorce rates, along with the higher marriage and fertility rates, of the 1950s are frequently proffered as proof of family values and often used as a comparison point when decrying today's families, it must be remembered that the conditions of the 1950s "Happy Days" were in fact unusual.[2]

Of course, not all Americans were experiencing equal levels of prosperity while this vision of family was being established. What seemed like a golden era for some communities felt like the dawning of the dark ages for others, including racial minorities, many European immigrant groups like certain Irish and Italians, and the abandoned people of the coal mining industry in Appalachia.

As the decades have gone by, some Christians have been firmly expressing their opinion that the family as an institution in America is breaking down and deteriorating. Some churches have responded to this concern with specialized ministries focused on marriage enrichment or working through the impact of, for example, divorce, extended adolescence, delayed marriage, same-sex attraction, single-parent homes, foster care, and multifamily and "nontraditional" households.

Certainly, challenging circumstances arise from experiences like divorce and children growing up in the absence of one or both parents. But have niche family ministries emerged in churches truly because of an actual breakdown of the American nuclear family? Or, perhaps, has our view of family for some time been overly narrow, even more so than biblical standards, amid a much more complex reality? Maybe what some consider "nontraditional" has always been more normal than we thought.

Maybe what some consider "nontraditional" has always been more normal than we thought.

Just as the first-century synagogue in Jerusalem was designed for Jewish families, the mid-twentieth century church had in mind the aspirational vision for the American household. However, the modern realities of the twenty-first century are forcing church leaders to grapple with what family looks like in a "Hellenistic" world.

The Modern American Family

Alongside the family sitcoms listed earlier is another list that reflects American life falling outside the aspirational vision of the American household:

- *The Andy Griffith Show* (1960–1968)—starring widower Andy, son Opie, and Aunt Bee

- *Sanford and Son* (1972–1977)—starring widower Fred, son Lamont, Aunt Esther, and Uncle Woody
- *Full House* (1987–1995)—starring widower Danny, brother-in-law Jesse, and best friend Joey, who helps to raise Danny's three daughters

These examples show that sitcom makers have been mindful to account for (and capitalize on) those who can relate to something other than the nuclear family. This is certainly true for *Modern Family*, which ran for eleven seasons from 2009 to 2020, earning eighty-five Emmy nominations and winning twenty-two.[3]

Modern Family focuses on Jay Pritchett,[4] the patriarch of the Pritchett family. Its episodes revolve around the interplay of three kinds of families: nuclear, blended, and same-sex. Jay, who is white and divorced from his first wife, DeDe, is now remarried to a younger woman, Gloria, who is Colombian and also divorced. Jay has a daughter and a son from his first marriage, Claire and Mitchell, and a third child, Joe, and stepson, Manny, from his second marriage. Claire is married to Phil Dunphy, and they have three children—one of their daughters, Haley, gets pregnant out of wedlock during the series. Mitchell, who is gay, eventually gets married to Cameron; the couple has adopted two children, both of Asian heritage.

The complexity of the Pritchett family may be exaggerated for entertainment value and comic relief, but their family arrangement is hardly unimaginable in twenty-first century American life. Currently more than half of first-time marriages end in divorce;[5] 23 percent of children live in single-adult homes;[6] the percentage of interracial, interethnic,[7] and interreligious[8] marriages is on the rise; and gay marriage is federally legalized.[9]

A substantial body of evidence suggests that while the social conditions of the mid-twentieth century offered one model for the modern nuclear family, many American households since then have not conformed to it, even if it was what they wanted. If there's anything worth learning for churches from sitcoms such as *Modern Family*, the key takeaway is that they have been too myopic on the nuclear family for their ministry programming. Church leaders should have also considered the dynamics of extended and nontraditional families so they could better engage the changing conditions of American family life. See, for example, the "family" changes reflected in Figure 3.1.

Figure 3.1—Dramatic Change in "Family" Image

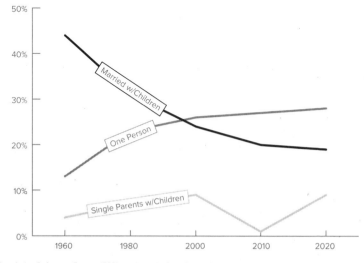

Population Reference Bureau (PRB), analyzed by Ryan Burge; image courtesy ECFA.

A few years ago, David Brooks, a well-known Canadian-born Jewish journalist who became a Christian in recent years,[10] wrote a long-form piece for *The Atlantic* provocatively entitled "The Nuclear Family Was a Mistake." As expected from the title, many considered Brooks's piece controversial, and some felt that it discounted the importance of the nuclear family. However, the article's main point focuses on the long-term effects of the decentralization of family upon society:

> If you want to summarize the changes in family structure over the past century, the truest thing to say is this: We've made life freer for individuals and more unstable for families. We've made life better for adults but worse for children. We've moved from big, interconnected,

and extended families, which helped protect the most vulnerable people in society from the shocks of life, to smaller, detached nuclear families (a married couple and their children), which give the most privileged people in society room to maximize their talents and expand their options. The shift from bigger and interconnected extended families to smaller and detached nuclear families ultimately led to a familial system that liberates the rich and ravages the working-class and the poor.[11]

Brooks frames the height of prosperity for nuclear families between 1950 and 1965, when it was most prominent in American history, past and present. He then argues that the conditions for this prosperity started to fade away toward the end of the 1960s, when many strains of cultural and economic distress began converging, eventually leading to the disintegration of many nuclear families, turning them into one of many other models for American households. Brooks's article is controversial because he often gives provocative commentary, such as the following insight:

People who grow up in a nuclear family tend to have a more individualistic mind-set than people who grow up in a multigenerational extended clan. People with an individualistic mind-set tend to be less willing to sacrifice self for the sake of the family, and the result is more family disruption. People who grow up in disrupted families have more trouble getting the education they need to have prosperous careers. People who don't have prosperous careers have trouble building stable families, because of financial challenges and other stressors. The children in those families become more isolated and more traumatized.[12]

While many in church leadership would not articulate their concerns in the same way as Brooks, it is not uncommon for pastors— especially of middle-class communities—to feel overwhelmed by the divorce rates among their church's membership, the complaints from aging or unmarried adults about how the church overly focuses on nuclear families, and the stale relationships church members have with others outside of the church, especially in their extended families and immediate neighborhoods.

These issues do not explicitly arise from the nuclear family. But there is some correlation—perhaps even causation—between the above-mentioned concerns and an overemphasis by American institutions on nuclear families to the detriment of larger family networks and structures, which are a part of the ecosystem that maintains healthy smaller units of family.

These "family" struggles that many church leaders face on a daily basis are certainly not enough for us to conclude with David Brooks that, sociologically speaking, the nuclear family is a mistake. But the problems are clear enough—even for those of us who affirm the importance of the nuclear family—that we need to reflect on two particular topics: the complexity of family ministry in the twenty-first century and the church's neglect of other structures for supporting family life in its programming and discipleship.

By the end of his article, Brooks is not contending for the abandonment of the nuclear family but instead desires to reimagine it rightfully in the larger context of extended family and what he refers to as *forged families*—meaningful long-term relationships developed amid a common experience (usually suffering or shared trauma).

Andrew T. Walker, associate professor of ethics and public theology at Southern Baptist Theological Seminary, offered a response to Brooks's article entitled "The Church as Forged Family," where he posits that the local church historically and in our day has been the place where forged family happens, "uniquely primed and, in fact, called to be the forged family for the unmarried, for single parents, and for the fatherless."[13] While the nuclear family is not necessarily an end goal or the idealistic model for church-as-forged-family, Walker maintains that it is the province from which extended family can be facilitated in congregational life. One illustration of forged family is the ministry represented by Faith City Church.

Faith City Church

A Minnesota Congregation Makes a Store Part of Its Mission

The Rev. Carl Johnson went from saying grace to selling groceries, turning a regular evening ritual into a way to address hunger in his St. Paul neighborhood close to the Mississippi River. "As we were praying, the words just started to shift after a while," he recalled of dinners with his wife Melanie Johnson, who is the worship leader of their Faith City Church. "We stopped praying about the meal that we were eating and started praying for others to have a meal."

Johnson owns Storehouse Grocers, the store he founded in 2019 that is now located in the same 2,200-square-foot space where his congregation of dozens gathers for worship, and where he also leads a cultural center for the residents of the Dayton's Bluff neighborhood of St. Paul.

Earlier in Johnson's ministry life, at a church in Lima, Ohio, he had worked to get meals and sustenance to hungry people through a food pantry and a soup kitchen. Once he arrived in Minnesota, Johnson, a former grocery store employee, helped distribute hot meals to hundreds of families.

At one point, Johnson determined that a store was the chief way to achieve his goal of halting everyday hunger. "We were ending hunger through hot meals and making sure families have three to five meals a week, and groceries were the next natural progression as part of our ministry," commented Johnson, who wears a black T-shirt that says "FAMILY MEMBER" in white letters. "When we say 'Church is not like family, church is family,' we mean that when you ask for help, we actually help."

The grocery store became what Johnson calls one of his Black-led multicultural church's "ports of entry." He views the store as an alternative to the traditional church food pantry and a way to help people consider the gospel after they've made other basic decisions in their life—including how they are going to access and afford their food. "If we're going to be decision-based people, how many decisions are people making before they make the decision for Jesus?" Johnson asks, calling addressing food insecurity "an expression of our church."

The community church also has a broad concept of family in scope and in meaning. It includes single moms, single dads, and multiracial families, reflecting the diverse neighborhood that comprises white, Black, Asian, and Latino people, as well as members of the Lakota tribe.

Johnson, 44, views his church's approach as an alternative to the sole way some churches seek to attain new attendees: through their front door for weekly worship. "Usually churches have one way: Sunday morning," he said. "But we have multiple ports. So we have a coffee shop and a cultural center. We do our outreaches, like the couple I'm doing premarital counseling for right now. I met them helping the homeless downtown."

The Storehouse Grocers volunteers, often from outside Faith City, also seek to connect with the customers besides ringing up sales and bagging their groceries. "We tell every volunteer to smile and tell a person your first name," Johnson said.

The people who have heeded that guidance include a young woman who had bought a house in the neighborhood, wasn't working, and had become the equivalent of the store's assistant manager. Other volunteers followed, including friends of Johnson's, their spouses, and members of other churches. "Our assumption was that church folk would come and volunteer and we'd be set," Johnson remarked. "But that assumption was completely wrong."

As he developed the church in partnership with more than a dozen congregations in the city, Johnson often mentioned the idea of volunteering at the store. But only a couple of people initially stepped forward. "We think a few reasons for this were that we were in a dangerous neighborhood, they didn't value what we were doing as volunteerism, and they just didn't find it attractive" to spend their time in that way, he explained.

The store aims to meet basic needs with flour, sugar, bread, eggs, milk, and canned goods. Cereal costs about $2, and Johnson aims to have no item priced over $5. He uses his retail handlers' license to buy and sell the groceries and uses the profits to pay for the expenses of the store. Johnson said he donates the remaining funds to the church. "We have a discounted rate that we get from the grocers," he commented regarding partners such as Hy-Vee, from which he purchases items that he, in turn, sells at his store to customers who can use their SNAP benefits to pay for the food that they need. According to Johnson, the store helps the church fulfill a "missional endeavor" by reaching "people who live in my neighborhood who are food insecure and are not affiliated with Christianity."

Johnson explained that when the church's worship service concludes, it segues into a time of fellowship where parents are invited to stay put and leave their children in a separate area so they can relax and "have a conversation for 10 or 20 minutes with somebody that's an adult."

The church's concept of "family" extends beyond the worship service and the grocery store. For instance, on its Facebook page the church referred to "one of our family members" when it held a fundraiser to assist her and her household in getting a new major appliance. Johnson had a friend who was able to give her one for half price, including installation and labor.

"We describe wealth as being able to get resources, and they needed our help, not just through financial resources but also through our connections with friends and family that can help them get the things done that they needed to do," said Johnson. "When we considered family, we thought of it as being a safety net in the community."

The cultural center, which is named after Black innovator George Washington Carver, is another outreach to the wider family in the community. "We hold open mic for Indigenous youth," Johnson explained.

"We have a Black business network meeting here once a month. We have created homeless panels here at our grocery store."

The discussions about homelessness included outreach workers and other people in the neighborhood who were knowledgeable about being unhoused and could share their perspectives in a safe place. After one gathering, Faith City began serving as a warming station for women and children.

The store's coffee shop features "free coffee Tuesday," which is another avenue to broadening the church's connections with its community. The church also offers the shop as a coworking space in the neighborhood, similar to other coffee shops across the country.

The grocery store—whose food products are the key step for reducing hunger—not only fills stomachs. Johnson said it also restores dignity to neighborhood residents, including the store's youngest customers. "Them being able to pick something off the shelf changes the power dynamic, in which they take control over their food choices," he elaborated, describing often heartwarming experiences as "one of the most beautiful things" about the store inside the missional church. "We would often see families come in with their children, and they would grab something off the shelf and their mom would not tell them to put it back."

The perspectives of the grocery store families are not the only thing transformed. The church members also see how a store allows them, through the church, to be a part of community transformation for those who have been food insecure.

"You find out that they are struggling with hunger in ways that you never would have guessed," Johnson observed, "but you can help."

The *Oikonomia* of the Early Church

While church leaders should pay attention to the cultural challenges when it comes to family formation and the development of community,

Scripture has already given us the language and ideas we need to evaluate how we could be falling short in this area and how we can live more into God's design.

In the New Testament, the church is called the *oikeios* or "household" of God (Eph. 2:19; 1 Tim. 3:15; 1 Peter 4:17). The Greek word *oikeios* derives from *oikos*, which ranges in meaning and translation from a home/house to a family/household. The notion "household of God" does not appear in an equivalent form in the Old Testament. While the Old Testament uses the family motif at times to describe the relationship between God and his people, conceptually the nation of Israel is hardly seen and understood as a household in the same sense as the church is in the New Testament.

The household concept for God's people emerged among Hellenistic Christians. This happened largely because the Greek social structure was developed around the larger unit *polis*, which was the city or public life, and the smaller unit *oikos*, which was the life into which someone was born or recruited.[14] The typical Greek household would have included extended family units, including bondservants and slaves, as well as the properties of the estate and business dealings. It was seen as a holistic unit of community encompassing more than just the nuclear family. This understanding of the church as an *oikos* was an adaptation made by Christians living in a Greek culture and using a preexisting Greek social construction.

In his book *Paul's Idea of Community: Spirit and Culture in Early House Churches*, Robert J. Banks makes a distinction between the churches started by the apostle Paul that met in homes and the traditional Jewish synagogues: "From a social and cultural point of view, Paul's communities, therefore, must be seen as part of a wider growth of voluntary groupings in society, in particular the development of religious fellowships within Judaism and Hellenism during that period."[15]

Viewing the church as a household frames how the early Christians thought of themselves corporately, as described in Acts 2:44–47:

> And all who believed were together and had all things in common. And
> they were selling their possessions and belongings and distributing

the proceeds to all, as any had need. And day by day, attending the temple together and breaking bread in their homes, they received their food with glad and generous hearts, praising God and having favor with all the people. And the Lord added to their number day by day those who were being saved.

Paul would go on to write about the qualifications of a church overseer in these terms: "He must manage his own household well, with all dignity keeping his children submissive, for if someone does not know how to manage his own household, how will he care for God's church?" (1 Tim. 3:4–5).

Within their skill sets and life experiences, church leaders in this context would have been able to deal with the complexities of an *oikos*—the *oikonomia* or economy—as a precursor to becoming overseers of the church. Paul prescribes that spiritual leadership is expressed through responsible management of the social, cultural, and economic development of an *oikos*.

Consider Lydia. While there is no indication that Lydia was an overseer of the church[16] that Paul started in Philippi, one can gain a greater appreciation for her skill as a "seller of purple goods" and the property she owned that became the first meeting place for the church after her entire household was converted and baptized (Acts 16:11–15, *oikos* in v. 15). Lydia's household—and perhaps even her estate—became the building block for the first church in the area that would eventually become Europe.

By way of analogy, church leadership in America from 1950 until now may have reflected more of a synagogue style of leadership found in Jerusalem. "Synagogue" leadership makes programmatic decisions from the top down, hoping unity comes through uniformity. On the other hand, "oikos" leadership seeks to facilitate unity from the ground up amid a

> Church leadership in America may need to reflect more of an *oikos* style of leadership, which facilitates unity from the ground up amid a lack of uniformity.

lack of uniformity. As we look to the next few decades, church leadership in America may need to reflect more of an *oikos* style of leadership in a Hellenistic reality that birthed churches in places like Philippi.

The Mixed Economy of American People

The *oikonomia*—the economy or management—of an American household has been challenged greatly by both cultural disruptions and innovations, leaving many church leaders feeling what Ross Douthat described during the COVID-19 pandemic as "Waking up in 2030."[17] This is the phenomenon of thinking that you had the luxury of waiting another decade or so before having to deal with a particular issue—and then struggling to accept that you might already be too late to get ahead of it. Understanding the main characters in Acts 16 may provide insight into the cultural and social challenges for how the church can build a more effective congregational life, now and for the future. Consider the following archetypes to guide our thinking.

The Macedonian Men

> And a vision appeared to Paul in the night:
> a man of Macedonia was standing there,
> urging him and saying, "Come over to
> Macedonia and help us." (Acts 16:9)

This archetype could represent cultural and institutional leaders—especially in sectors such as education, health, and community development—that need renewal. Like the Macedonian man, they are asking for help to improve the fate and future of their communities. They are often gatekeepers and shopkeepers, ready to transition their organizational models from synagogue to *oikos*. They are also strategists who have exhausted the best practices for engaging both traditional and nontraditional families. They are now realizing that their limitation isn't a lack of skill or willingness but a generational and cultural gap that can't be overcome, especially by tactics and policy. Regardless of their politics and positions on a particular issue, these leaders are finding themselves at the helm of a ship with little fuel and a stuck rudder, wondering how they can navigate their communities through the most polarizing events of their lifetime.

The Lydias

> One who heard us was a woman named Lydia, from
> the city of Thyatira, a seller of purple goods, who was
> a worshiper of God. The Lord opened her heart to
> pay attention to what was said by Paul. (Acts 16:14)

This archetype could represent the gifted, talented, and spiritual people who creatively meet by the riverside in addition to the synagogue. Like Lydia, they would not fit the profile for synagogue leadership. They are achieving all the metrics of success and happiness typical to an American family but perhaps without having a nuclear family of their own. They don't feel comfortable in either the church's marriage or singles ministries. But they could get used to religious environments if we help them reimagine their existing social environments under the lordship of Jesus. These people need someone like Paul, who not only provides sound teaching content but who also helps them to rethink their own social spaces. The Lydias of today may be the most fertile ground for seeing new and agile expressions of church emerge.

The Lydias of today may be the most fertile ground for seeing new and agile expressions of church emerge.

The Oppressed

> As we were going to the place of prayer, we were
> met by a slave girl who had a spirit of divination and
> brought her owners much gain by fortune-telling.
> She followed Paul and us, crying out, "These men

are servants of the Most High God, who proclaim
to you the way of salvation." (Acts 16:16–17)

This archetype could represent the prophetic presence of the most vulnerable and oppressed in society. These have the least standing in any social space to which they belong (if they are in one at all). At best, they are condescended to and caricatured by traditionalists and progressives alike because they are so far outside the norms of society. At worst, they are demonized and discarded as the ones ailing society. They often lack compassion for themselves because of the weight they carry alone and the callousness they have developed as a survival mechanism. It is difficult to design resources and ministries with them in mind because their presence is perceived as having marginal impact by those in control of most organizations.

The Jailers

When the jailer woke and saw that the prison doors were
open, he drew his sword and was about to kill himself,
supposing that the prisoners had escaped, But Paul
cried with a loud voice, "Do not harm yourself, for we
are all here.". . . . And he took them the same hour of the
night and washed their wounds; and he was baptized
at once, he and all his family. (Acts 16:27–28, 33)

This archetype is different from the powers-that-be because such people are the rank-and-filers who need empathy and security. They see a significant power distance from decision makers and institutional leaders, and wonder if American organizations—including the local church—are headed in the right direction. They would almost never comfortably be in the same social spaces as the Macedonian Men and the Lydias. These people are traditionalist in the way they think about family and community, but, often, their extended family and maybe even their own nuclear family are "falling apart." Today, more than ever, blue-collar white men are being conflated with the powerful in America, and are pushing back against this narrative. A sobering reality is that, according to the American Foundation for Suicide Prevention, the rate of suicide is highest among middle-aged white men.[18]

The zeitgeist of our time wants to drive the wedge deeper between the diverse economies of people and households in America. But just as the Spirit of God worked through the apostle Paul and his band of missionaries in Macedonia, our time demands a missionary church that preaches a gospel robust enough to bring change at the private, personal, and public levels of people's lives. Ten years after Paul initially visited Philippi, he looked fondly back on the church he started there that successfully integrated disparate groups of people into a new forged family. He could say, "I thank my God in all my remembrance of you, always in every prayer of mine for you all making my prayer with joy, because of your partnership in the gospel from the first day until now" (Philippians 1:3–5).

Integrating Congregational, Community, and Civic Life

We are not suggesting that the aspirational vision for the American household described at the beginning of this chapter should change or that it will go away. The physical expressions of institutions develop over several hundred, if not thousands, of years and cannot easily be thwarted or modified in just a few generations. However, we do want to acknowledge that the advent of the twenty-first century has brought a need for churches to investigate their paradigms and programming, which have become heavily reliant on the social conditions that shaped their particular vision for family.

Many American communities are no longer reflective of traditional, nuclear families but rather of forged families. At the same time, we also acknowledge that local churches cannot and should not try to accommodate any and every whim of culture. Deep and authentic communities by nature cannot accommodate absolutely everyone.

Still, the churches of the future will have permeable lines between the rhythms of congregational life and the rhythms of the community that surrounds them. They will become more integral to civic engagement and community development, and will also have the opportunity to adapt to newer and more complex social issues than the ones familiar to previous generations. The church leaders of the future will help Christians understand that the church cannot be all things to all people but that it can still be more things to more people. They will also help Christians understand better where to get the necessary support—whether inside or outside of the church—to feel secure in their unique family configurations and personal affinities.

> The churches of the future will have permeable lines between the rhythms of congregational life and the rhythms of the community.

The *oikos* illustration reminds Christians not to make the church the center of life for someone, per se, but rather encourages them to see God's work through their church as a facilitator—and maybe an organizing principle—for their lives. The church promotes integration between a person's layers of personal identity (personal, private, family) and public identity (congregation, community, civic). This perspective empowers Christians to have agency and autonomy to find additional communities that can support and complement what is missing from their congregational life. This may include supporting a person belonging to more than one church for a season, or maybe even for an indefinite period. It also removes some of the burden and guilt church leaders often feel when they are unable to provide niche ministries. To say it another way, churches of the future will find ways to complement and be complement-able with other groups also in the business of creating places of belonging.

> Church cannot be all things to all people, but it can still be more things to more people.

Church leaders that embrace church as *oikos* will not obsess over having members and potential members conform to a 1950s American ideal for family. While not ignoring the Bible's affirmation of the nuclear family, church leaders of the next few decades will cast a vision and develop a mindset among their churches' members to see boundaries expand beyond just Sunday services and midweek programming. Their ministry will spill over into the places where the Macedonian Men, the Lydias, the Oppressed, and the Jailers are experiencing the traumas of life, forging them together into a new household of God.

One Degree of Change

Next are simple statements adapted from various ideas presented in this chapter about different kinds of families and communities. Use the scale below each statement to assess how much you agree with it, choosing one answer for each row. Then begin some leadership conversations by comparing how much your responses align with the outlook of others in your church. There is space at the bottom of each list item for you to jot down any thoughts or ideas.

1. The "family" makeup of our church is likely to dramatically change in coming years.

☐	☐	☐	☐	☐
STRONGLY DISAGREE	DISAGREE	UNCERTAIN OR NO OPINION	AGREE	STRONGLY AGREE

2. What some consider "nontraditional" families (as described in this chapter) are more common than our church typically addresses.

☐	☐	☐	☐	☐
STRONGLY DISAGREE	DISAGREE	UNCERTAIN OR NO OPINION	AGREE	STRONGLY AGREE

3. Whatever our church's "family ministries" become, they need to create more places of belonging for those who seek to follow Christ.

☐	☐	☐	☐	☐
STRONGLY DISAGREE	DISAGREE	UNCERTAIN OR NO OPINION	AGREE	STRONGLY AGREE

4. Our church is willing to serve all four of the Acts 16 archetypes named in this chapter—the Macedonia Men, the Lydias, the Oppressed, and the Jailers.

☐	☐	☐	☐	☐
STRONGLY DISAGREE	DISAGREE	UNCERTAIN OR NO OPINION	AGREE	STRONGLY AGREE

5. The Lydias of today may be the most fertile ground for seeing the emergence of new and more agile expressions of church.

☐	☐	☐	☐	☐
STRONGLY DISAGREE	DISAGREE	UNCERTAIN OR NO OPINION	AGREE	STRONGLY AGREE

CHAPTER 4

From Mind to Soul

WHY THE FUTURE IS BIRTHING A NEW APOLOGETIC

Dated question: How do we convince unchurched friends to develop more interest in eternal things?

Better question: How can we enter more people's pain and show them the God who cares?

THE TREND: Proclaiming truth not by winning an intellectual debate but by showing and sharing how the gospel heals social and spiritual trauma.

Shift #3: *The gospel's credibility depends on both the message and the messenger. Going forward, most discussions about the gospel will first need to address the skepticism or apathy triggered by the listener's distrust and previous experiences. In the past, giving a clear explanation of the gospel was often enough to lead someone to become a Christian who already believed in God or had a Judeo-Christian ethic. However, skeptics were asking questions such as:*

Does God exist?

Why does God allow bad things to happen to good people?

What about the problem of evil and suffering?

Are science and faith compatible?

In recent decades, these topics have garnered substantial crowds on university campuses across America, especially when framed as a debate between an atheistic professor and a well-known Christian apologist. Anyone who has ever attended this kind of event probably would have heard the atheist give a reason from his or her field of expertise against some theist position or an aspect of the Christian faith. The rebuttal from the apologist may have included counterpoints with rational and intellectual arguments that appealed to agnostic listeners. It was also common for the apologist to assert core tenets of the Christian faith during the course of the debate and give reasons for why Christianity is distinct from other religions and worldviews. If hosted by a Christian campus group, this event was intended not mainly for the apologist to win the debate but primarily to gather an audience of people who might never attend a church. This occasion would give the undecided an opportunity to hear essentials of the Christian faith, especially from an intellectual framework.

It is difficult to say if the effectiveness of these events is permanently waning or if they will surge again and reach an even greater audience than in previous decades. In what was one generation's heyday of campus Christian apologetics in the 1990s and early 2000s, atheist intellectuals such as the "Four Horsemen"—Christopher Hitchens, Richard Dawkins, Sam Harris, and Daniel Dennett—represented the "offense" that necessitated the kind of "defense" provided by apologists like J. P. Moreland, William Lane Craig, Lee Strobel, and—before he became known for scandal and a mired past—Ravi Zacharias, just to name a few. At that time the Christian faith was squaring off with a postmodern and increasingly post-Christian America.

Why were these presentations effective? Many of the Gen Xer and millennial university students targeted by these events—if they were American—likely would have come from boomer-led families whose parents had at least some Christian heritage. Boomers in America grew up during a time when belief in God was at a high point. As a result, these kinds of questions at the turn of the twenty-first century would make sense to them, and perhaps even to their children, because they remembered a time growing up when it seemed that everyone believed in God. The boomer worldview was predicated on the existence of God more than any generation that followed.

> The boomer worldview was predicated on the existence of God more than any generation that followed.

Gallup has tracked Americans' trend in belief in God every year since World War II. Its first recorded data in 1944 indicated that 96 percent of Americans had a belief in God—which would have largely meant a Judeo-Christian God. At this belief's height in 1953, 98 percent of Americans would have said they believed in God. However, by 2022 that percentage dropped to 81 percent. When looking at 18- to 29-year-olds, that percentage is dramatically lower: only 68 percent. Today, one out of three young adults in America has no belief in God.

> Today, one out of three young adults in America has no belief in God.

Across all categories, ideological liberals between 2013 and 2022 have experienced the highest drop of those who have a belief in God, at –11 percentage points.[1]

However, these percentages are even more troublesome than the fact of mere decline because the 19 percent of all adults who indicate no belief in God is the highest percentage in history since Gallup began tracking this data. Furthermore, the conception of "God" today, especially among young people, is much broader and more diverse than just the God of the Bible.

In order to understand the magnitude of the 19 percent, as of the writing of this book, extrapolating this percentage would mean that nearly 50 million American adults in 2024 might indicate no belief in God,[2] compared to around 2.2 million in 1953. To put that number into perspective, this would mean today that there are almost as many American adults who do not believe in God as the total number of people living in South Korea, which is 51 million, and more than the number of people living in Spain, which is 47 million. That's the combined population of the entire states of Texas and New York! Clearly, this increasing group calls for new approaches in our apologetics, as Figure 4.1 affirms.

Figure 4.1—Rapid Rise of "No Religion"

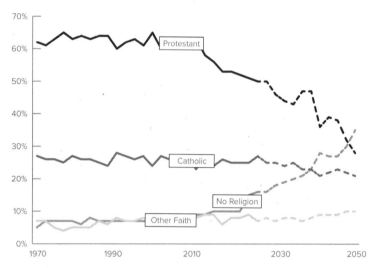

General Social Survey, 1972–2022, with extrapolations 2023–2050; image courtesy ECFA.

From Post-Christian Rhetoric to a Postmodern Cry

How did it happen that in just two generations, the United States went from a nation where almost everyone believed in God to a nonbelieving America that is larger than the average population for all countries in the world? The answer reveals some major shifts in assumptions, in the questions people care about today, and in the fallout from how Christians behave amid their controversies.

Of course, something this vast and complex goes hand in hand with many other trends, such as declines in church membership and attendance (see chapter 2), increased confidence in evolution and science to explain life's mysteries, a broadening religious pluralism, the loss of social stigma toward people who say they don't believe in God, and a skepticism or loss of confidence in religious institutions. Other factors include immigration from increasingly atheistic regions such as China and post-Soviet and Western European nations.

Moreover, the high percentage of people who no longer follow the faith of their parents is especially pertinent for today's religious climate. We can no longer assume that people will remain in the faith traditions of their birth. People switch (or abandon) faiths for many reasons. One of these triggers traces back to the great schism among Protestant denominations—often referred to as the fundamentalist–modernist controversy—and the assumption that the categories it created are relevant to today's generation.

> We can no longer assume that people will remain in the faith traditions of their birth.

Much ink has been devoted to this schism, which catalyzed at the dawn of World War I. Included in this era of American Christianity were events such as the Scopes Monkey Trial of 1925, the splintering of Presbyterians followed by other Protestant denominations, and a movement to rethink foreign missions in the context of humanitarian efforts rather than evangelism and conversion. But two related issues lay at the foundation of the schism: the debate over the views of Scripture and essential Christian doctrines and the reinterpretation of church traditions to accommodate modern ideals. Theological liberals were willing to compromise with culture because their understanding of the authority of Scripture continued to evolve. On the other hand, theological conservatives were willing to battle with culture because culture had changed. By the time the Second World War was over and the project of nation rebuilding was underway, conservatives had separated themselves to develop their own institutions and to put feet to their vision for a more Christian America.

As the dust of the schism was settling, America had two main factions of Protestant Christianity: the fundamentalists and the modernists. Today, the largest stream among the fundamentalists mostly identifies as conservative evangelicals, while the largest among the modernists identifies as liberal mainliners. Although the schism was seen as mostly theological, it had major implications for the social, political, and institutional landscape of America in the twentieth century. The schism not only created a trajectory but also spawned a worldview for the way many Christians would defend their faith and define their churches and organizations for decades to come.

Some church leaders today feel that while the schism is over, the war against secular culture and liberal theology is not. If the 1950s were the golden era of Christianity in America for many, then, in these leaders' minds, churches today exist in a post-Christian era amid a culture war, where both American culture and American Christianity are consequently being fought over by those on the ideological left and right.

George Marsden, professor emeritus of history at the University of Notre Dame and an expert at the intersection of American culture and Christianity, writes about how the culture wars reveal something about the liberal–conservative/left–right dichotomy:

> The often strident debates over moral and political issues that emerged in the late twentieth century came to be known as culture wars, and these would continue into the twenty-first century. Yet, despite their diametrically opposed stances on many issues, *commonalities could also be found* between the ideological left and the ideological right, even if neither side acknowledged these common traits. Both sides, for instance, were remarkably individualistic. Americans typically insisted on believing what they wanted and had a negative view of the authority of institutions. Many people on both sides talked of personal fulfillment and favored expressive individualism that valued intense personal experience. Both sides, despite professions to

the contrary, tended toward materialism, often defining values in terms of availability of material comforts and security. Both sides were largely comfortable with the benefits and the pleasures of technological society, although ironically the religious right was often less critical of relying on technology than the left. Both sides were, in their own ways, moralistic, insisting that certain sorts of beliefs and behavior were unacceptable and hoping to legislate their standards for the whole society.[3]

For decades, many church leaders felt that the war and defense (apologetics) for orthodoxy and orthopraxy in America were fought on a dichotomous plane, under terms of engagement that—when looking from the outside—would seem antithetical to the Bible and in opposition to Jesus's teachings about the kingdom of God.

Figure 4.2—Share of Nonreligious Homes More Than Doubled Over Last 40 Years

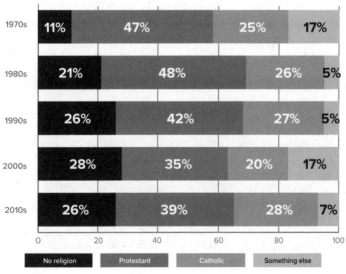

General Social Survey, 1972–2018, analyzed by Ryan Burge; image courtesy ECFA.

For example, liberals and conservatives alike are willing to demonize or caricature the other side to strengthen the commitment of their base. Many conceded that they were engaging their opponents in a very different manner from Jesus's teachings on the Beatitudes in Matthew. Often,

> **Liberals and conservatives alike are willing to demonize or caricature the other side to strengthen the commitment of their base.**

they were not poor and meek in spirit, hungering and thirsting for righteousness, but instead could not act mercifully with pure intentions. Thus, perhaps the culture wars did just as much to reveal that while some feel America is becoming post-Christian, others felt churches and church leaders behaved, and maybe even became, un-Christian. These culture wars seem to be one of many contributors to the growth of nonreligious homes, as Figure 4.2 demonstrates.

Questioning Assumptions

Meanwhile, as new generations arose, the issues they care about have changed—and even the way they frame the issues has shifted. As a result, church leaders today are still fighting over questions from the fundamentalist–modernist controversy while their youth—along with other seekers and skeptics—are moving on to other questions. For example, one question they are asking is: How should Christians behave amid their controversies?

Rachel Held Evans, born in 1981, was a *New York Times* bestselling author who died after a brief illness in 2019 at the age of thirty-seven. Evans was a Christian who initially identified as evangelical but later became Episcopalian. While much of Evans's writings critiqued the evangelical tradition in which she grew up and the religious right in America, many evangelical leaders still eulogized her, especially because she gave voice to her generation of Christian youth in the church who were filled with questions and doubt. Ed Stetzer, the dean of Biola University's Talbot School of Theology, wrote about her for *Outreach* magazine:

What Rachel did, and what so many others in our churches are (sometimes silently) doing, is more common than most know: She questioned what she had been taught and what she was seeing.

Doubts, questions and concerns are part of every believer's life, whatever form that takes and at whatever stage of life.

Watching the reaction to her death has reminded me that our churches need to be a safe place for people who wander and for people who wonder. . . .

The last few days I've been asking: What must our churches do with the questioners—whom some may call "the wanderers"? . . .

Yes, Rachel Held Evans stirred the evangelical pot in ways that were uncomfortable and distressing. However, for me, she made me think and she made me better. She pointed out my logical fallacies and forced me to defend my assumptions.[4]

Evans grew up in Dayton, Tennessee, the very town that had held the Scopes Monkey Trial. She even wrote a book about her perspective on Christian fundamentalism, provocatively entitled *Evolving in Monkey Town: How a Girl Who Knew All the Answers Learned to Ask the Questions.* Some might consider Evans part of the postmodern church movement in America. She even admitted in her bestselling book *Searching for Sunday: Loving, Leaving, and Finding the Church,* "I used the word *postmodern* a lot."[5] *Searching for Sunday* chronicled Evans's journey as a millennial growing up in church, struggling with doubt largely due to the culture wars, and eventually accepting the church with all its flaws. In a series of essays published posthumously in *Wholehearted Faith,* Evans writes:

It would be dishonest for me not to say I am a Christian when Christianity is the story I will wrestle with forever. There's something about Christianity—and by that, I mean the venerable, beautiful story that has Jesus at its center—I just can't shake. And I don't just mean the parts I like, or the parts that on good days I believe. I mean the whole thing. The whole screwed-up, embarrassing, dysfunctional family of the church is as much a part of my identity as my gender, my nationality, my ethnicity, and my name.[6]

While Evans remained in the church, many in her generation did not find any defense compelling enough to stay. She and the doubters for whom she was providing a voice remind us that the robust Christian faith needed for the future will not be boxed in by the rules of engagement for the last century. Whether one agrees with Evans on her views and theology, upon reading her body of work it is easy to see that she was offering a genuine caution to church leaders that a large swath of America's emerging generation cannot be conveniently labeled as conservative or liberal. Forcing them into these categories might force them out of the conversation.

> **A large swath of America's emerging generation cannot be conveniently labeled as conservative or liberal.**

The framework of the fundamentalist–modernist controversy is no longer robust enough to support the questions and the angst of the emerging generation. Some are apparently longing for an enchanted and transcendent story of the world that makes sense if someone like Jesus—or a group modeled after Jesus—is radically at its center. The most compelling communities of faith for those weary of the American cultural wars are informed of the culture but not consumed by it. They provide places of compassion and empathy while retaining healthy tradition and conviction.

The post-Christian rhetoric could very well be the historical backdrop of this generation, but it may not be where they choose their battles. We see examples of this situation play out in the recent hashtag movements of the last decade.

How Hashtag Movements Helped and Hindered the Church

Here are some recognizable online hashtags associated with social movements that have recently challenged many of America's institutions:

- #MeToo
- #BlackLivesMatter
- #WomensMarch
- #OccupyWallStreet

And then, of course, there are some hashtags specific to Christians and the church:

- #ChurchToo, #SBCToo, #PCAToo, etc.
- #EmptyThePews
- #Exvangelical
- #WeirdChristianTwitter

These are just a few of the more prominent movements. At their essence was awareness, advocacy, and activism for a hurting population; social pressure to bring change to a system; and healing for individuals and their loved ones. Hashtag movements are different from other kinds of social campaigns because they have the ability to quickly reach a broad audience due to the virality of social media platforms. Hashtags also allow virtually anyone without qualification or relevance to the issue to speak publicly about it without being in an in-person format or organized environment. These kinds of people can include online trolls but are often genuine individuals concerned about a matter.

The #MeToo movement is a classic example of how a hashtag movement became a disrupter in almost every American institution. Tarana Burke founded the "Me Too" movement in 2006, years before the hashtag went viral. Burke had experienced sexual assault and wanted to help women and girls—particularly those of color—who had also survived sexual violence. She wanted the world to know how prevalent sexual assault against women and girls was, and she desired women and girls to know that they were not alone in their experience. Burke's entry into advocacy work started when she met a thirteen-year-old girl she calls "Heaven" at a youth camp in Alabama, who confided about her assault to Burke. This humble start as a grassroots movement would become a trend a decade later as #MeToo on social media in 2017.[7]

Soon enough, industries and institutions from Hollywood to large Christian denominations experienced an unveiling of stories from women and girls who had experienced sexual assault or harassment, often at the hands of organizational leaders. #ChurchToo and other denominationally specific hashtags would soon follow as stories from Christian women and girls emerged about abuse.

Other hashtag movements have unique but parallel origin stories. For instance, the #exvangelical hashtag started by Blake Chastain[8] is similar to Rachel Held Evans's journey. It became an online movement of mostly millennial Christians leaving the church because of their doubts, questions, and incompatible views on certain theological and social issues. #EmptyThePews, initially calling Christians to leave churches that supported extreme Christian nationalism, was started after the 2017 Unite the Right rally in Charlottesville, Virginia, a meeting of alt-right, neo-Confederates, and neo-Nazi groups.[9] And while the origin of #WeirdChristianTwitter is not as clear, this movement has become a forum of sorts for Christians to share their sometimes comical but at times painful upbringing and life moments in the church.

Of course, not all churches have been affected by these movements, whether Christian or broader campaigns. Additionally, many churches across America have likely been oblivious to their existence. But it is hard to imagine that a majority of churches in America has escaped grappling with the social phenomenon undergirding these hashtag movements: an unjust system covering up or even perpetrating the harm that specific groups of people have experienced.

> **Believers and skeptics alike need places in which they can safely tell their own stories of hurt and pain.**

Pastors and church leaders have had to navigate this difficult conversation over the past decade in higher degrees than ever before during their lifetime. And whether or not they can successfully detach the causes for abuse away from their theology and polity, they will have to show and defend that what they believe from the Bible is not a part of the harm but is in fact part of the healing.

Believers and skeptics alike need places in which they can safely tell their own stories of hurt and pain, receiving empathetic attention from Christian listeners. They also need spaces where they can ask authentic questions grounded in their own experience. These needs have elevated the role of a different type of apologetic, as the following story illustrates.

Coastal Church

CANADIAN CONGREGATION EVANGELIZES A DOWNTOWN WITH FEW CHURCHGOERS

Pastors David and Cheryl Koop were told it couldn't be done: birth a church in a neighborhood of Vancouver, British Columbia, where less than 3 percent of the community described themselves as churchgoers.

"We had individuals, well-meaning individuals, say that would not be the place to start a church," Cheryl recalled. "And we felt that that would be the place the Holy Spirit would want, because there were needs there."

Leaving behind careers in the oil industry, the Koops cofounded Coastal Church in 1994 about four blocks away from the Pacific Ocean. The church's location lay among glass-walled, high-rise buildings in the heart of downtown Vancouver.

"There wasn't this congregation or group of believers to start with us," Cheryl said. "It was us and a couple of other people that felt the same way."

The leaders of the church that had begun with just a few who believed in its future eventually discovered that small groups were the path to the congregation's growth. Coastal Church now averages three thousand people attending services in person on weekends across ten physical locations, with approximately seventy nationalities represented.

Though the Koops were convinced that the community needed a new church, the local people were uninterested in Coastal Church's first attempts at evangelism in the city center, which was filled with banks, law offices, and universities.

"There was an intentional and extensive program in phoning individuals and sending material to introduce ourselves, letting them know that a church was coming to the area," Cheryl remarked concerning the "Phones for You" campaign. "I think out of the 12,000 phone calls, we had four people that showed up for our first worship service."

"None of them came back either, by the way," added David.

Likewise, a campaign to share the popular *Jesus* film of Cru (formerly Campus Crusade for Christ) also proved to be fruitless—despite efforts to get the VHS tapes into apartment buildings. (Remember, this was still the mid-1990s!)

Then, in 1996, the church tried something else: Alpha. This ten-week evangelistic course bills itself as featuring "no pressure, no follow-up and no charge." It was originally created by Nicky Gumbel, a former lawyer and recently retired London-based Anglican priest who thought it would be a good idea to hold a series of sessions about the basics of Christianity in a nonjudgmental way that invites people to voice their honest opinions about it.

The Coastal Church volunteers who serve as facilitators of Alpha are ready to share about their Christian faith in the weekly conversations but are instructed beforehand to be open to whatever is said in this safe setting as participants watch short videos and discuss the Bible or their impressions of Christianity.

"The facilitator is to say, 'That's interesting,' not to say, 'That's wrong. The Bible doesn't say that. You've got it wrong,'" Cheryl said. "No, they're just instructed to say, 'That's interesting' and then pass the ball to someone else in the group: 'What do you think about that?'"

Leaders hope to add to the comfort level of attendees by sharing food—originally fancy meals served on china—and fellowship on every occasion the small groups meet. "They said, 'make it a wow,'" said David, 67, regarding advice he received on how to make the course, which now has a simpler look, a great experience for participants. "Wherever it is, we give it the best. If it's pizza, then let's order the best pizza. Wherever we're setting up, it has to be the best we can present in that context."

Whether people eat on paper plates at a church location, high schoolers dine on pizza, or organizers add "a nice touch" to a gathering at a high-rise building's common room, the Koops emphasized that the need they meet during these gatherings is key. "The number one need in our city is loneliness," said David. "One of the reasons Alpha works is because it's a meal and there's small groups."

Cheryl, 66, said that the fellowship and learning that come during the two-and-a-half-month course are punctuated by a weekend away where openness to the Holy Spirit is a dominant element of the program's success. She remarked that "those relationships don't stop" when the regular weekly meetings officially conclude, since gatherings often continue at nearby coffee shops.

The groups that meet for Alpha include people of a mix of faiths, experiences, and ages, although people in their 30s tend to predominate. According to the Koops, some may have been raised in Hindu, Muslim, Sikh, New Age, or gnostic traditions, but they often are no longer practicing the faith of their birth. More have no religious affiliation, reflecting about 50 percent of people in Vancouver.[10]

David commented that a number of the people of other faiths sometimes explore Christianity for the duration of the course and then move on. "However, most of these people are very open to receiving Christ and most of them will," he asserted regarding those who had been born into religious homes but weren't practicing. "We would see more people coming from a secular background to faith than people coming from other religions, because that's more of what we have in our community."

The end of an Alpha course is often the beginning of next steps for the participants, with some continuing to ask questions, some becoming Christians, and others joining the church or taking part in service projects that help people in locations from the Yukon Territory to Ukraine.

Over the years, about three-quarters of Coastal Church's congregants have been involved in small groups, many of which are called Life Groups. These people meet weekly for discussion of the Bible or recent sermons, for prayer, and to support one another in times of crisis.

Some apprentices—volunteers who help facilitators lead the Alpha course—move on to lead Alpha and other small groups themselves. Some may follow what the church calls a "leadership pipeline" where they first serve as volunteers, then become leaders, then coaches and ministers. A few of them go on to pursue master's and doctoral degrees.

Church attenders and members with no church background who may not be ready for or interested in a leadership track may take the Alpha class over—and over—again, remarked David. "They will do Alpha sometimes three times just to understand the basics: Why the Bible? Why Jesus? Why the resurrection? Alpha's been the starting point for their journey in faith, and it's helped them get the ABCs."

Cheryl explained the church's "come and see" approach to evangelism that echoes words from the first chapter of the Gospel of John. "Why don't you come with me?" she said, reiterating the question church members can use to invite friends and family to an Alpha course. "And then we say, 'Then you commit to those ten weeks to be with your friend or loved one. And you sit with them in those small groups, not to preach to them but just to be there alongside them.'"

Cheryl views Alpha as training of the most important kind. "We educate ourselves on everything else, but we don't educate ourselves on eternity," she said. "So, why don't you educate yourself on this and then you make the decision, after ten weeks, about what your final viewpoint will be?"

Alpha can help reduce misinformation, too. David noted that the Alpha organization had found through a survey that young people aren't questioning the existence of God. Rather, they are asking, "Is God good?"

"They discover that some of the information they had about Christianity or even religion wasn't accurate," David continued. "When they discover the beautiful Jesus and discover God's good in community, that's a big part of the ethos that makes Alpha work. They then come to faith in Christ."

David recalled one attendee summing up the Alpha course at its conclusion: "I found the beautiful Jesus."

Embodied Gospel Healing

The effectiveness of groups such as Alpha is likely to grow in scale because, by nature, these gatherings are attuned to the individual questions and needs of their participants and can be catered toward a local church's vision. These groups will endure as a simple and basic tool for churches to do their job of easily creating simple, nonthreatening spaces for seekers and skeptics to ask questions. Additionally, their renewed focus on youth and culturally contextualized versions of their curriculum will almost ensure their usefulness and relevance for the future.

The last few years have also seen an emergence of new apologetic platforms such as Lisa Fields's Jude 3 Project (J3P). J3P has become a preparatory movement for "black voices trained in conservative and progressive spaces to discuss important topics for the church and culture."[11] Its 2023 national conference highlighted seminars and topics covering questions such as: *How do I heal from church hurt? Is Christianity good for black people? How should my faith inform my politics? How do I reconstruct my faith after doubt?* The emergence of J3P affirms the future need for churches to contextualize apologetics to the lived experiences of actual people in their community.

The leadership skill of creating empathetic and conversational spaces is increasingly important for the Christian defense in the twenty-first century. For some, the answers to *Does God exist?* or *Why does God allow bad things to happen to good people?* lie in how church leaders are able to address and handle the harm experienced by vulnerable people in their congregation and in their community. The issues of the twenty-first century are testing the strength of the church as a holistic and healing body.

The apostle Paul writes about this in 1 Corinthians 12:22–26:

> On the contrary, the parts of the body that seem to be weaker are indispensable, and on those parts of the body that we think less honorable we bestow the greater honor, and our unpresentable parts are treated with greater modesty, which our more presentable parts do not require. But God has so composed the body, giving greater honor to the part that lacked it, that there may be no division in the body, but that the members may have the same care for one another. If one member suffers, all suffer together; if one member is honored, all rejoice together.

Paul is making an argument by way of an analogy. He is making a case for the value and equality of all people within the church. His greater point here and in the chapters that follow in 1 Corinthians is that the health and witness of the church is predicated on its ability to appropriately honor and care for those who, according to society, might be overlooked and forgotten based on worldly standards. When the "parts of the body that we think less honorable" are not being honored and cared for, the church will stand up for them rather than ignore them.

In the tradition of Jesus's teachings, Paul is arguing that the church is the place where people find healing, belonging, and a kind of honor they would not otherwise receive. "If one member suffers, all suffer together." This is perhaps the most difficult but also the most prominent opportunity for the defense of the gospel and the Christian way—that a group of people might suffer with you as if it is their own suffering. Indeed, that was the way of Jesus in his crucifixion.

Just as Jesus embodied our suffering for our healing, the church's greatest defense of the gospel in the twenty-first century will be its role as a place of embodied gospel healing.

Christian psychologist and trauma specialist Diane Langberg has many times prophetically challenged the witness of the church in our day amid a watching world with this statement: "Trauma is the mission field of the twenty-first century." She explains in her book *Suffering and the Heart of God: How Trauma Destroys and Christ Restores*:

> The trauma of this world is . . . one of the supreme opportunities before the church today. Our Head left glory and came down to this traumatized world. He became flesh like us; he literally got in our skin. He did not numb or flee the atrocities of this world or of our hearts. Will we, his body, also leave our spaces, our chapels and enter the trauma of terrified and shattered humanity in the name of Jesus? We are complicit with the perpetrators if we refuse to see and enter in. We are also complicit if we go ignoring the refuse in our own hearts. If the church does not enter in, then I would ask, is she really living as the body of an incarnated God? How I pray we will follow our Head, full of the light and life of Jesus Christ in the corners of our own hearts *so that* we might truly bring him to the trauma dungeons of this world.[12]

You do not have to discount the rational questions people have regarding the existence of God and the intellectual stumbling blocks toward faith in Christ that they struggle with. The apologetic of the American church now and for the foreseeable future will be both head on *and* hands on. We must have wisdom and appropriately enter into people's trauma in order to learn their history of pain, loneliness, and abandonment that is often the source of their skepticism. The callousness of doubt is sometimes covering the tenderness of a wound. Naturally, it is cruel to peel back someone's

The apologetic of the American church now and for the foreseeable future will be both head on *and* hands on.

doubt without being willing to tend to this person's wound. The rational reasons for God may begin to emerge the moment someone's suffering begins taking on meaning. More precisely, meaning is discernable and discoverable in suffering, especially when experienced with others in community.

> **Meaning is discernable and discoverable in suffering, especially when experienced with others in community.**

If we become a trauma-informed church, we are not adopting a framework of moralistic therapeutic deism, which sees religion in America as mainly a pathway for moral living, feeling good about oneself, and reverence for an impersonal God.[13] Moreover, we are not attempting to substitute treatment and services that therapists and psychologists are professionally trained to provide. Along with the rest of society over the past few decades, the church has grown in both its understanding and response to trauma. It is now applying science-informed methodologies and approaches to its purpose of creating safe communities for its members. The church is applying Paul's theology of the spiritual body as expounded in 1 Corinthians 12 to the physical body as understood in the twenty-first century. Therefore, the mission of making a disciple of Jesus Christ should, from now on, include processes and spaces where people understand more about the pains of their past so that they can discern how the gospel is able to heal their present and future.

Participation and Presence

Some church leaders in the presence of nonbelievers are tempted to always or only see apologetics as a means for evangelism and conversion. Indeed, this call to "teach" Jesus's good news is unquestionably and biblically warranted, a necessary part of his commission to his followers (Matt. 28:19–20).

However, the combination of deed and word is only one dimension of giving a defense for the Christian faith. Adding another dimension—participation and presence—can broaden Christian witness without losing its evangelistic purpose. Meaningful presence can do even more to bring out the many processes and pathways toward mission as deed and word.

To understand the value of this concept for Americans today, imagine that you and your family, who follow Jesus, have moved into a neighborhood where almost everyone else is part of a different religion. Maybe they're Muslim, Hindu, Sikh, or Hasidic Jewish. They trust each other, but not you. They have all kinds of family, social, and employment networks, but you're not part of these. They have a certain perception of Jesus that is possibly negative and inaccurate, but their view is truth to them. However, these people, like you, also have hurts and pains in life—broken relationships, loneliness, abandonment, disappointments, fears, and dreams. How do you enter their world?

The following diagram in Figure 4.3 is a proposed model[14] through which churches and church leaders can participate with God in an ongoing process of Christian witness among a skeptical community. Its axes

Figure 4.3—Witness as Mutual Exchange of Word and Deed

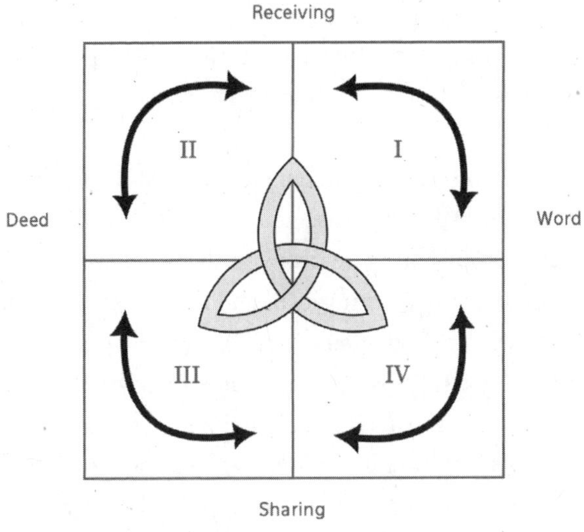

Model and image developed by Daniel Yang.

represent the deed and word component of Christian witness as well as the component of presence indicated by sharing and receiving.

Quadrant I: While there is no set starting point to enter into participation with God in Christian witness, receiving a word from a non-Christian partner is an easy and humble first step. Receiving the word can mean learning from others about their belief, theology, lifestyle, or even personal spirituality. It can also mean experiencing something together with them that may or may not have religious significance.

Quadrant II: Here Christians are also in a receiving posture. However, they are receiving not just words and knowledge but also deeds of service, favors, and anything else that creates a relational obligation to the other. Here, presence is deepened and Christians show themselves to be vulnerable. They are needy, and it does not immediately place them in a place of power and influence.

Quadrant III: Now the Christian is reciprocating with deeds of service and favors. Sharing a deed shows both a desire for a relationship and the willingness to bring something tangible to the relationship. Understandably, there is also a risk of rejection here. However, sharing is a necessary part of gaining trust and building friendship with the non-Christian partner. This is being a witness to Christ in presence and should never be part of a bait-and-switch scheme.

Quadrant IV: Sharing a word with the non-Christian, of course, entails not only evangelism and a defense of one's faith but also wisdom and often correction. Verbal proclamation of the gospel and witness to Christ is an essential part of apologetics. Christians who never engage in this form of dialogue likely lack conviction or are being overwhelmed and inundated by their non-Christian partner.

In this model, Christians are never meant to operate only in one quadrant. Nor are they expected to stay in one mode for a very long time. In fact, a natural progression from one mode to another shows mutuality and respect and indicates that a trusting relationship is likely forming. The process of apologetics as participation and presence aligns with the idea of intentionally entering into people's pain in order to serve them both in deed and word.

> The process of apologetics as participation and presence aligns with the idea of intentionally entering into people's pain in order to serve them.

Adjusting Your Posture for Better Proclamation

New terms and phrases have been developed to describe today's rising generation, such as "spiritual but not religious." This generation's pain priorities of anxiety, loneliness, and alienation are very different from the emotional felt needs of previous generations. Instead of looking to pastors and churches for answers to life's questions, members of this generation search Google and talk with friends. They will also likely talk to a therapist before contacting a church leader. That is not an indictment on the former as much as on the latter. Finally, the questions and issues that matter most to this generation are usually a far cry from the way earlier generations thought.

However, do not mistake the different approach needed going forward as a lack of receptivity to the Creator of the universe and the all-powerful gospel of Jesus Christ. We just need to find new ways to access people's trust, minds, and hearts.

Furthermore, just as missionaries in a foreign culture would understand the importance of presence, relationship, and vulnerability in their evangelism, so likewise this outlook is needed in America today. In this day and age, the safe church is an effective evangelist and a strong apologetic. Its leaders must be vulnerable about their own needs and shortcomings. They need to be trauma-informed and trained to listen and to receive. This is a posture, not just a proclamation. It is a different method, but it still serves the same unchanging gospel.

One Degree of Change 4

Next are simple statements adapted from various ideas presented in this chapter about a new apologetic to serve people not only in deed and in word but also with presence and participation. Use the scale below each statement to assess how much you agree with it, choosing one answer for each row. Then begin some leadership conversations by comparing how much your responses align with the outlook of others in your church. There is space at the bottom of each list item for you to jot down any thoughts or ideas.

1. **We need to explore more types of apologetics, especially ones that don't assume the other person believes in God.**

☐	☐	☐	☐	☐
STRONGLY DISAGREE	DISAGREE	UNCERTAIN OR NO OPINION	AGREE	STRONGLY AGREE

2. **We're sensing that the fundamentalist–modernist categories of conservative and liberal don't resonate with the rising generation and might even cause them to drop out of the conversation.**

☐	☐	☐	☐	☐
STRONGLY DISAGREE	DISAGREE	UNCERTAIN OR NO OPINION	AGREE	STRONGLY AGREE

3. The church's greatest defense of the gospel going forward is to become a place of embodied gospel healing.

☐ STRONGLY DISAGREE ☐ DISAGREE ☐ UNCERTAIN OR NO OPINION ☐ AGREE ☐ STRONGLY AGREE

4. The role of apologetics is increasingly one where posture matters, not just proclamation, and where the attitude and awareness of the speaker matters, not just the content of the proclamation.

☐ STRONGLY DISAGREE ☐ DISAGREE ☐ UNCERTAIN OR NO OPINION ☐ AGREE ☐ STRONGLY AGREE

5. The average members of our congregation look for ways to share their faith with others.

☐ STRONGLY DISAGREE ☐ DISAGREE ☐ UNCERTAIN OR NO OPINION ☐ AGREE ☐ STRONGLY AGREE

6. The average members of our congregation know how to meaningfully share their faith with others.

☐ STRONGLY DISAGREE ☐ DISAGREE ☐ UNCERTAIN OR NO OPINION ☐ AGREE ☐ STRONGLY AGREE

CHAPTER 5

From Church Refugees
to Church as Refuge

WHY TRUE HOSPITALITY IS ESSENTIAL
FOR CONGREGATIONS TO THRIVE

Dated question: How can we stay a "big happy family" by reaching more people like us?

Better question: How can a culture of irresistible hospitality unify our congregation's increasing diversity?

THE TREND: Mitigating division not by avoiding conflict but by creating truly hospitable places that allow people to be seen and heard.

Shift #4: *Conflict has always happened in local churches, but in the past the factors of community homogeneity and theological tradition were usually strong enough to prevent deep division in the congregation amid larger cultural tensions. However, in recent years much of society's glue that formerly reinforced church bonds has been loosening. Consequently, going forward, churches must develop a new depth of hospitality—far more than an usher's*

*welcome or a cup of coffee after worship—or their people won't
experience genuine unity . . . and perhaps won't stay long enough
to develop it.*

Conflict can absolutely kill a church's momentum and vitality. Research affirms a direct relationship between conflict and decline in a church.[1] As society becomes more diverse, fracturing and splintering in churches will sadly become more common. Too many churches think—wrongly—that they can be protected from division by avoiding conflict or by working only with people whom they can uniformly agree with ideologically. Avoiding conflict often ends up looking like one generation leaving behind difficult and increasingly complex issues for the next generation to inherit. Such avoidance may work in the short term, but fissures and tension points will inevitably emerge, paralleling any surfacing polarities in our culture.

> **As society becomes more diverse, fracturing and splintering in churches will sadly become more common.**

What is a current signal that too many churches aren't handling conflict well? Every week in America, people whom researchers call church refugees[2] shuffle in and out of various congregations—sometimes discreetly but at times loudly (usually online by posting or blogging about it)—hoping to find a new spiritual safe house to rest and heal.

Church refugees aren't casually on the market looking for a different and more exciting church. They aren't disgruntled religious consumers who complain about the length of a sermon, the volume of the music, or the quality of the children's programming.

Instead, more often than not, church refugees are genuine and committed Christians looking for respite from a trauma-inducing division that they or others experienced in church or within their denomination. Most recently, during the COVID-19 pandemic these refugees influenced many congregations either to grow or to shrink and even close their doors.

Many church refugees loved their church dearly and never imagined uprooting from a community that they spent years serving and building. But they ultimately concluded that staying in their current church was untenable. They once saw themselves as "lifers," but now find themselves stuck in a perpetual transitional pattern of noncommittal church attendance.

The reasons why committed people leave are as diverse as the people themselves, but two common factors are almost always present: personal tension and churchwide conflict.

To say it plainly, almost no people leave a spiritual community they dearly love unless they feel the tension has reached an unmanageable boiling point. By contrast, churches that deal openly with conflict tend to be healthier, as Figure 5.1 affirms, and happier too! (The term "vitality" was self-defined by survey takers, who were asked the extent to which they agreed or disagreed with the statement "Our congregation is vital and alive.")

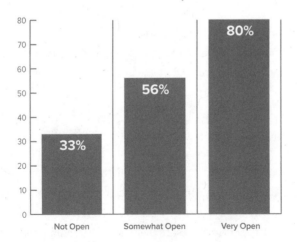

Figure 5.1—High-Vitality Congregations Address Conflict Openly

Comparison of High-Vitality Congregations

"Insights into Congregational Conflict," Faith Communities Today, 2019, Figure 4, p. 3; image courtesy ECFA.

There has always been faction-ing, splintering, and splitting during the entire history of religion and the church. However, each generation experiences division in a way that is unique to its time and culture—which has never happened before—so the solutions of the past can't conveniently and simplistically be applied today.

We can learn tremendous lessons about church strife from the New Testament, such as in Acts 5 (Ananias and Sapphira), Acts 6 (Grecian and Hebraic widows), and Acts 15 (the Council of Jerusalem), and from historic events such as the split of the Orthodox Church from the Catholic Church and the Protestant Reformation. But the descriptions of these significant divisions are not direct prescriptions to modern church leaders for how to handle #BlackLivesMatter, critical race theory (CRT), debates over masking and vaccinations, the 2020 presidential elections during the COVID-19 pandemic as well as in 2024, or today's debates around gender identity and sexual orientation. American church division in the twenty-first century isn't better or worse than in previous eras, but it also isn't the same. In fact, the surface issues that characterize our modern tensions have never existed anywhere else in the history of the church. Therefore, we need to understand the historic social conditions leading up to our modern cultural moment in order to effectively apply biblical principles for achieving church unity.

The Big Sort 2.0

After analyzing U.S. Census data and demographic trends of American neighborhoods and drawing on alarming data and ideas from sociologist Robert G. Cushing, journalist Bill Bishop argued in his 2009 book *The Big Sort: Why the Clustering of Like-Minded America Is Tearing Us Apart* that people continue to sort themselves into homogenous communities. Bishop shows that the growth of megachurches, specifically in the suburbs, is typical of the appeal of homogeneity. While people in the past tended to attend churches with others who were most like them or reflected the lifestyle they wanted for themselves, Bishop maintains that the more recent era of sorting caused American churches to become more culturally and politically segregated than their neighborhoods.[3] This was especially true of the 1980s seeker-sensitive churches that were started in American suburbs. Two decades later, the rise of churches using the language of multiethnicity was an attempt to address the effects of the "Big Sort" on churches.

Bishop interviewed renowned American church historian Martin Marty, who observed that churches had once been built around a geographic community but were now constructed around similar lifestyles. Marty bemoans:

> A huge element in retention of loyalty and acquisition of new church members can be summarized in a very simple phrase: a choice of a way of life. . . . I've always argued that what society needs are town meeting places where people with very different commitments can meet and interact. Churches have been that [in the past]. If you're a Methodist and you move to Des Moines, Iowa, and you get to the nearest Methodist church, thirty or forty years ago you would have an open encounter. People who were pro-Bush or pro-Kerry would talk. Fertilization would go on. Now it simply doesn't happen.[4]

Church leaders today are working against forces that have been in motion since the Cold War and Jim Crow eras. These forces have morphed and integrated into newfound forms and outlets, such as cable news and social media. The unease that many church leaders feel during this particular time of polarization in American history is an indicator that the Big Sort isn't over yet and is driven more by ideology than theology. The COVID-19 pandemic perhaps catalyzed or fast-tracked this generation of sorting as churches divided over masking, the response to racial protests, and the results of the 2020 election.[5] In some ways, churches experience the same tensions that other institutions face, but they may pretend to have a different way of handling division or possibly are unable to see that they've taken the same approaches as secular or non-Christian institutions. To sum up, ideological homogeneity may be easier in the short run, but it develops intolerance in the long run.

The "How" and "Why" of Divisive Issues

The effective church leader for today and tomorrow will need to know how to navigate through socially and politically divisive times with an appropriate knowledge of the controversial issue's historical context. Understanding why members think the way they do is important to addressing their concerns and decisions. After all, member behavior is often at the root of congregational conflict, as Figure 5.2 shows.

It is not enough for leaders to know only *what* is being debated by Christians. Right now, and especially for the future, leaders critically

Figure 5.2—Member Behavior Top Source of Congregational Conflict

Category	Percentage
Members' Behavior	44%
Money	42%
Worship	41%
Leadership Style	40%
Decision Making	39%
Program Priorities	30%
Theology	26%

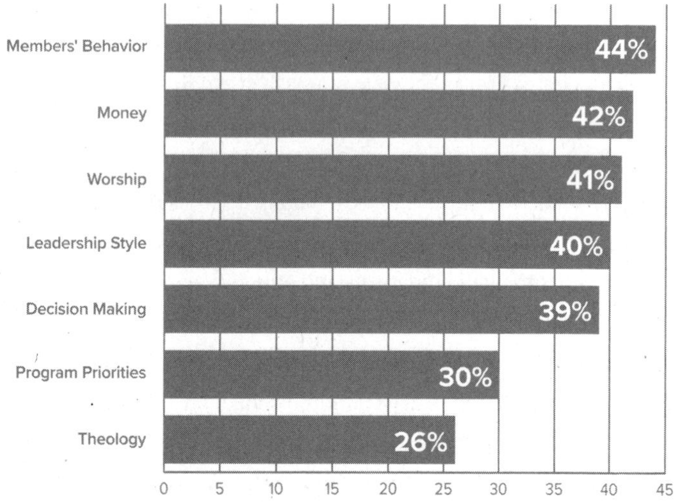

"Insights into Congregational Conflict," Faith Communities Today, 2019, Figure 2, page 2; image courtesy ECFA.

need to know *how* these things happened in history and *why* they are being debated in the public square. Otherwise, they may fail to disciple their members to grow in both knowledge and empathy, to better understand root issues, and to approach opposing perspectives with grace, humility, and good intentions.

Take, for example, the especially pertinent issue of U.S. border security and immigration policy pertaining to undocumented immigrants. In 2024, Lifeway Research conducted a survey, jointly sponsored by the Evangelical Immigration Table and World Relief, to ask how evangelicals felt about current U.S. immigration issues and policies. Most respondents—80 percent—indicated that they would back bipartisan immigration reform to strengthen border security, establish a pathway to citizenship for undocumented immigrants who came to the U.S. as children, and provide a reliable number of screened, legal farmworkers. Additionally, 2 out of 3 evangelicals (65%) said that they would be more likely to vote for candidates who supported such "immigration reforms."[6]

This would seem to indicate that many Christians have a positive disposition toward undocumented immigrants. However, some cable news networks and other media outlets regularly portray Christians as universal supporters of "closed borders" and the repatriation of all undocumented immigrants. While certainly some Christians may feel this way and, in the past, influential Christian figures have even supported the halting of immigration,[7] Christians have always been on all sides of this issue.

Whatever their perspective on this issue may be, discerning Christian leaders will need to understand, if they don't already, that the history of immigration policy in America has been a mixture of good and bad decisions—mostly driven by economics, but sometimes by xenophobia.[8] They will also need to understand the background behind why some Latin American migrants continue to make the difficult decision to journey toward the southern U.S. border. The book *Migration and Public Discourse in World Christianity* helps Christians better understand this historic context: a lot of migration is a consequence of America's involvement in Latin America during the Cold War and its role in the development of banana republic governments.

> The US intervention in all these conflicts, in the form of military training, financial support to regimes that favored US interests, or directly guiding local elites to overthrow democratically elected leaders that represented a potential or actual threat to US interests, has been amply documented. This strategy of direct or indirect intervention always implied economic interests, and it took different forms, the latest being the free trade agreements that were signed under the argument that they would help the development of the Latin American countries. As part of these free trade agreements, many assembly plants were established in Mexico and Central America, taking advantage of low wage rates.[9]

As the economic conditions in these countries worsened along with their own governments, the U.S. became the most natural place for Latinos to seek refuge because of its long-term involvement and partial responsibility. As Latino American residents of the Southern states have often said, "We didn't cross the border; the border crossed us."

If church leaders don't take time to understand the historic context for this issue, as well as for other pertinent social issues, they will be tempted to allow the popular media to dictate why and how they facilitate conversations among their church members and how they engage their neighbors. While understanding a historic context doesn't mean advocating for a particular side of an issue, it can help set the tone and give perspective for why such matters are much more complex than they first appear.

Social Conditions in the Antioch Church

Understanding a little bit more about why and how America's neighborhoods and communities sorted the way they have can help church leaders navigate the consequences of the Big Sort. They can avoid creating intolerant and tone-deaf communities caused by extreme homogeneity and follow in the steps of the very first Christians, who practiced such avoidance.

If there was ever a context in the Bible where Christians were going to misunderstand each other socially and culturally, the church in Antioch would most likely fit that scenario. A new social group that had never been seen before in that part of the world had been developing within an urban context. It was so different that a new name had to be given to describe it; Acts 11:26 indicates that the followers of Jesus were called "Christians" for the first time in Antioch. This local moniker would later be adopted globally because there was something unique about this Antiochian church, in part because there was something unique about Antioch itself.

In *The Rise of Christianity*, Rodney Stark titles its seventh chapter "Urban Chaos and Crisis: The Case of Antioch." A city like Antioch would have been known for its social chaos and chronic urban misery due to waves of newcomers from non-Greco Roman cultures and the fracturing of the local culture into numerous ethnic fragments and enclaves.[10] As a sociologist, Stark reflects on the cultural turmoil of this cosmopolitan city to better understand the social conditions that formed the church there:

> Any accurate portrait of Antioch in New Testament times must depict a city filled with misery, danger, fear, despair, and hatred, . . . a city filled with hatred and fear rooted in intense ethnic antagonisms and exacerbated by a constant stream of strangers. [It was] a city so lacking in stable networks of attachments that petty incidents could prompt mob violence.[11]

While most American cities are likely in better shape today than first-century Antioch, from a sociological perspective the dynamics of present-day America are closer to Antioch than to first-century

Jerusalem. The groups of people that eventually formed the church in Antioch did not have a common origin, nationality, or way of life. While "Jesus is Lord" was their simple and common creed, learning to work through their differences and divisions wouldn't have been easy. The church in Antioch wasn't just the coming together of individuals but a collection of a myriad of worldviews that had developed from politically and historically distinct civilizations.

The people of the church in Antioch created space for one another despite their differences and uncommon origins. They would have also created this space despite political affiliations, for even one of their leaders, Manaen, was "a lifelong friend of Herod the tetrarch" (Acts 13:1).

Antioch stood out from among the other churches as an exemplar because it became the home church for Paul and Barnabas on their missionary journeys. The heterogeneous nature of the church in Antioch created a robust culture that became the launching pad and home base for the church's first missionary endeavor into the rest of the Gentile world. While the Holy Spirit's outpouring at Pentecost had occurred in Jerusalem among the Jews and Jewish converts, Jesus's global commission for his followers to go into all the world to make disciples of all nations (Matt. 28:19–20) seemed to unfold more from Antioch.

However, the Antioch church's vibrant culture was not developed without tension and division. Galatians 2:11–14 records a sharp dispute in this church between the apostles Paul and Peter (named there as Cephas). In that environment, the apostle Peter had been comfortable eating with Gentiles. However, because some Jewish converts sent from the apostle James had visited the church in Antioch, Peter was no longer eating with Gentiles for fear of legalistic Judaizers—what Paul referred to as "the circumcision party." Peter's shift eventually led more Jewish converts, including Barnabas, to also abandon eating with Gentiles. Dangerously, these Jewish believers were reverting to their old ways and igniting fear-based narratives in a culturally divided city and within a church that had a reputation for reconciling rivals.

To some moderns, the idea of fighting about eating together may seem like a small and insignificant dispute, even when we understand the deep history of Jewish kosher food laws. But community and trust are often built over food and drink in ancient and collectivistic cultures all around the world today. In anthropology, "commensality" is the act of intentional eating together for the sake of building relationships and creating and maintaining culture and customs. Eating together wasn't merely symbolic of peace and harmony among a people; it was often a *means* for attaining peace and harmony.

> Community and trust are often built over food and drink in many cultures around the world today.

Peter's decision to break commensality with his newfound brothers in Christ who were Gentiles signaled to the rest of the group that their previous cultural and ethnic ties were more important than the new divine ties created in faith. Commensality was hospitality at the highest level, and because of fear and shame the Jews in Antioch gave into their ethnocentrism and broke fellowship. Restoring commensality would necessitate deeper theological conviction in the gospel so that it could be practically applied, such as in sharing daily life activities together and welcoming one another into homes and to meal tables. This would be a key refrain of Paul's epistles to the Gentile churches.

A More Robust and Practical Theology of Hospitality

True hospitality goes far beyond what visitors experience from friendly ushers when they attend a worship service for the first time. It also goes beyond the level of care offered through small groups and benevolence ministries. At the heart of hospitality—both practically and theologically—is an ongoing posture of how people in a congregation give to and receive from one another, as modeled by the Trinity and the humblest versions of the church

> At the heart of hospitality— both practically and theologically—is an ongoing posture of how people in a congregation give to and receive from one another.

throughout history. Hospitality is the feature and character of the church that allows individuals and families to nurture their belonging in the community in their ongoing commitment to something outside of themselves. When people can no longer comfortably decide what they give and receive in community, and when church leaders can no longer discern who is and isn't being welcomed, the culture of hospitality is nonexistent. As this chapter's opening discussion of church refugees illustrated, people leave places when they no longer feel visible, even if they once called these places home.

We should not develop a practical theology of hospitality primarily because we want to address or avoid conflict. Rather, hospitality is a covenantal posture that both individuals and the corporate body maintain because it is intrinsic to the way of Jesus. He embodied a life that welcomed the stranger and made room for people with diverging backgrounds and perspectives. This is how he led his first disciples. A quick rundown of the Twelve (Matt. 10:1–16)—with backgrounds as fishermen, political extremists, tax collectors, and more—reminds us that Jesus could have been just as comfortable (or bothered) by Christians from the right and the left of the political spectrum. But wouldn't people from both sides have been invited by him to sit at his table? And both groups would have been challenged by the life to which Jesus called his followers to live. Hospitality facilitates the working through of differences and challenges.[12]

In her seminal book *Making Room: Recovering Hospitality as a Christian Tradition*, Christine Pohl asserts that hospitality is what establishes and reinforces social relationships and moral bonds. She underscores that hospitality is most noticed when socially undervalued people are welcomed and recognized.[13]

At the root of division and tension is our fear of being invisible and being replaced by another. We often think division happens when a person is misunderstood. That is usually the case on the surface; however, a closer look at why someone or some group is consistently misunderstood and misrepresented reveals that this almost always happens because this person or group is unseen or overseen. In contrast, the belief and practice of hospitality ensure that all groups present are seen, recognized, and welcomed. A hospitable outlook is also mindful of inviting relevant groups that are not yet present.

Inhospitable environments do not have well-articulated pathways that allow people to offer affirming or diverging opinions. Instead, their leaders often deliver top-down decisions that are cloaked with theological jargon, political maneuvers, and cowardly pragmatism. When this happens, people in the most vulnerable group usually see church leadership as siding with an opposition (which is often seen as an aggressor) and negating their voices, twisting their thoughts, and leaving them invisible. In those cases, the church leadership becomes a second point of conflict. Thus, the boiling point before people leave usually occurs when they feel neglected or begin opposing church leadership.

At other times, churches publish theological stances or policies on a particular social issue without having any long-term relationships with the people most affected by the issue. Public statements are sometimes necessary to show solidarity, but they can be hollow at best or perhaps confusing when a church has never shown any real attempt to know and understand the people behind the issues. A posture of hospitality normalizes the clunkiness of not immediately having to say the right thing by putting people and relationships first. It recognizes that policies serve people, not the other way around. Over time, a culture of hospitality leads the church to be preoccupied with caring for people's real needs more than curating its public image.

> A culture of hospitality leads the church to be preoccupied with caring for people's real needs more than curating its public image.

Hospitality does not mean that all groups will always get what they want in every situation. But a church that has this posture ensures that every group—and, whenever possible, every person—has an avenue to express fears and desires when they arise. People feel exposed and vulnerable when expressing need. Therefore, when they do express their concerns, a church leadership that is capable of empathetic and active listening and appropriate action needs to give them full attention. Hospitality is a posture toward people, not a position on a policy. It keeps relationships accountable and makes accountability relational. In the case of Mosaic Church, hospitality kept the congregation moving forward amid a tumultuous and divisive time.

Mosaic Church

HOSPITALITY OVERCOMES HOSTILITY AT OHIO CONGREGATION

While tens of millions watched their broadcast news outlet of choice as the votes in the 2020 presidential election were being cast, Mosaic Church held a daytime Communion service in downtown Dayton, Ohio.

"On the day of the presidential election, we bring folk together. No matter your side, no matter whom you voted for, we're going to be 'one'," said Rosario "Roz" Picardo, a co-pastor of the United Methodist church in Beavercreek, a suburb of Dayton. "We're going to be the church of Jesus."

Picardo also preached on unity during this time of year, when the country might seem most divided, urging people to vote but never saying how to vote or endorsing candidates, even as his congregants posted on social media about their favorite choices. "Our citizenship is in heaven, first of all—we're dual citizens," said Picardo, 44. "Our mantra is John 17: that we are one, that God calls us to be one, and that we are better together."

The "Better Together" slogan—worn with the words in English and four other languages on an in-house T-shirt—expresses the team approach of the church Picardo founded in 2017 with Wayne Botkin that now includes Lilanthi Ward as a third co-pastor.

"We're multiethnic and multi-income," Picardo said of the church where Arabic, Spanish, Korean, and Portuguese are spoken by attendees. "We have white collar, blue collar, and no collar. We're a recovery church as well." Picardo himself is a Sicilian American who was involved in "cultural Catholicism" early in his life and then raised as a teen in Pentecostal Christianity.

The church, attended by about six hundred people each week, offers a variety of worship services, including traditional, acoustic, Spanish, and recovery. The last type of service includes dinner before a Wednesday evening gathering featuring the Serenity Prayer and "clean time shoutouts" by people who are grappling with addictions to alcohol, drugs, sex, or gambling. "Hey, I've been ten days sober," or "I've been two years sober," Picardo has heard people say. He has also heard, "Hey, I got my kids back. Hadn't been able to see my kids."

Picardo says his church models the 70/30 philosophy he learned about from his colleague the Rev. Chip Freed of Garfield Memorial Church, a United Methodist congregation in Cleveland. "Seventy percent of what we say and do, you're going to love, but you're going to hate 30 percent," he said. "But your 30 percent is someone else's 70 percent and vice versa."

Picardo admits that the option of a traditional worship service isn't his favorite, but he still preaches at that service during his once-a-month preaching rotation. Likewise, he and other Mosaic staffers seek to help members of the congregation find ways to cooperate despite their differences.

Picardo acknowledges that sometimes the church isn't always successful. For instance, during the height of the COVID-19 pandemic, Mosaic Church lost and gained attendees as it made decisions about masks and in-person worship. The church also experienced tensions during the period of protests following the death of George Floyd under the knee of a Minneapolis policeman. At that time, Picardo clearly affirmed the statement "Black lives matter."

"We lost the people we needed to lose during that season, but we still grew," he commented, "and so it takes a posture of humility and listening on our part but also hearing from our brothers and sisters—our nonwhite brothers and sisters, as well."

The church has striven to be intentional in the diversity of its worship and its conversations. For example, it held a multiethnic conference in 2023 that continued the church's "Better Together" theme. Those discussions have also included some of the elderly members of the small white congregation that Mosaic Church adopted when it moved into a permanent building after previously meeting in movie theaters and school buildings.

"When you do things like Be the Bridge or you have multiethnic conversations, it's just interesting who shows up and who doesn't," Picardo said. "A majority of our folks stick with us, even if they have disagreements, or they're growing, or they may not understand things. But they know Christ is being lifted up and they feel the Holy Spirit in worship: 'Hey, this is going to be my home.'"

Picardo acknowledges that some find those kinds of conversations difficult—so tough that they may choose to leave the church. "It doesn't mean that people don't get mad at each other," he said. "It doesn't mean that the wrong thing is not said. Because sometimes it is. And, so, how do we address that? How do we help people? How do we all grow together?"

Picardo also recognizes that some people depart because they are more comfortable in a homogenous church. He considers humility to be a "prerequisite" as the church's members strive to work through racial and political tensions by having difficult conversations, which are sometimes fostered by outside organizations with expertise in overcoming divides. "I have to see you. You have to see me," he summed up. "We have to be willing to listen to each other."

As the church seeks to keep people together who come from a range of backgrounds and viewpoints, Picardo said he wants more than front-door evangelism that helps newcomers over the threshold. He seeks an approach that gets people to stick around, join small groups, and worship with others who may not look like them or live like them.

Picardo said he has studied the Walt Disney Company's efforts to make people welcome at their parks. For example, his church doesn't call out visitors or make new people stand up because those supposedly welcoming gestures may make some of them feel uncomfortable. The intangible ways of making people feel a part of Mosaic, he believes, are more effective than having a food court or other expensive amenities in its building.

In the end, Picardo sees hospitality as Mosaic Church's most important attribute. "I hate using the word 'customer service,' but having that stellar customer service is huge," he said. "You could tell me, 'Hey, the preaching wasn't great.' You can tell me, 'Oh, the music was too loud.' But don't tell me that we were an inhospitable congregation."

Spaces That Cultivate Staying Power

Just like in a family, hospitality is really about valuing and preparing those who already belong so they can readily practice help and responsibility toward others. Otherwise, there is nothing to welcome others into. Hospitality is centripetal in nature: upon experiencing it, people tend to gravitate toward the center of the community. This is a movement toward deep and authentic relationships that is difficult to achieve on a mass scale and in a short timeline. While it is possible to invite a lot of people to the table quickly, it is very difficult to make sure that everyone who shows up feels heard and valued and has what is necessary to take part in decision-making.

In order for people to feel safe and confident to work through conflict and division in a community—especially on sociopolitical and ideological issues—they need to have a sense of long-term welcome and staying power. Staying power is not developed just by listening to preaching or attending a membership class. Rather, it develops over time when people work through conflict. But, paradoxically, people are less likely to deal with conflict if their long-term relationship to the group is at risk.

One of the authors of this book, Daniel Yang, has spent the larger part of the last decade leading and consulting in multiethnic churches and networks among various theological traditions, helping leaders create spaces empathetic to underrepresented groups. Through his various consultations, he has discovered that there are four dynamics that people need to experience within a church, as visualized in Figure 5.3, in order to feel welcomed enough to work through adversity:

Visibility—"I feel well-represented and seen in this church."

Voice—"I feel able to appropriately express myself openly and freely in this church."

Value—"I feel able to experience vulnerability and accountability in this community."

Volition—"I feel able to exercise choice and can affect how those in power make decisions."

Figure 5.3—Keys to People Enduring Adversity

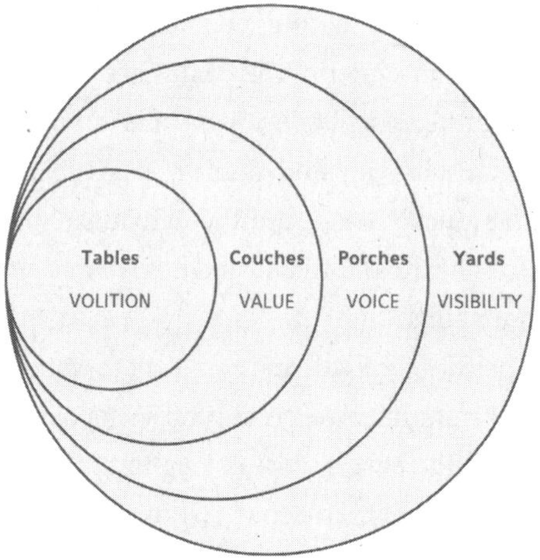

Tables — VOLITION
Couches — VALUE
Porches — VOICE
Yards — VISIBILITY

Model and image developed by Daniel Yang.

When any of these four things are at risk, a person's staying power is destabilized. Consequently, leaders should regularly reflect on where and how these dynamics are being intentionally cultivated in the rhythms and cadence of the church, as well as how these dynamics are or are not being experienced by church members. The church leader who is think-ing about the future must consider the places and spaces where people are strengthening these aspects of their church experience.

Historically, the church relied on catechesis, member classes, con-gregational meetings, small groups, and other spaces to cultivate some of these dynamics. While these spaces have been important for assim-ilation purposes, they have not necessarily led to cultivating the skills necessary to deal with conflict. Thus, churches of the future will need to develop new intentional spaces that will nurture the four dynamics just mentioned—spaces that will help their people navigate complex conver-sations. For example:

> **Yard Spaces.** These are forums and gatherings where people dia-logue around the theological, social, and cultural constructs that contribute to identity and society structures. They are normalized and easy-access spaces where people can continue to engage cultural issues with their faith and feel assured that this dialogue is a regular part of church life, not antithetical to it. Examples of yard spaces can include charitable seminars or webinars that utilize conversational frameworks and ground rules that allow participants to speak freely, safely, and maybe even imperfectly in order to hear and to learn from one another.

> **Porch Spaces.** People often need safe spaces that are not overly regulated or curated where they can work out their questions and doubts on an issue and express their thoughts, even if these are still imprecise. Porches and foyers are beautiful because they allow people to process doctrinal and social issues without having to fully reflect the core beliefs of the church. Examples of porch spaces are classes or cohorts that allow people to "check out" the theological and philosophical foundations of a church, simultaneously giving church leaders a forum to learn and understand how they can make their community more accessible.

Couch Spaces. Similar to church small groups or life groups, couch spaces are a familial-type structure that allows people to discover their most authentic selves, as God intended. These groups don't have to be the most accountable for someone's spiritual life, but they could be the intersection of pastoral care, recovery from life trauma, and opportunities for people to give to others from their own experience. Examples of couch spaces can be less programmatic versions of well-known organizations, such as Stephen Ministries, Celebrate Recovery, or Christianity Explored, which allow someone to journey in a community designed for spiritual discovery and soul care.

Table Spaces. Ultimately, the most welcomed people will want to make decisions within the community for themselves and for others. Table spaces are made especially for those who are trying to help others feel welcomed and to stay. But they are also the well-articulated spaces and pathways for people to raise concerns when the church at large seems to be straying from its mission and purpose. Examples of table spaces are leadership pathways and advisory councils that are proving grounds and onramps for future church leaders who will replenish, revitalize, and represent various church constituencies.

Unity in the twenty-first century will be experienced by church leaders who are able to discern between problems to be solved and tensions to manage.[14] These problems and tensions can be addressed only if there are regular ways to acknowledge and bring them to light. Perhaps one of the most urgent assignments for this generation's church leaders is to innovate spaces that honor people who are committed to faith and community but who also have different experiences and perspectives.

One Degree of Change 4

Next are simple statements adapted from various ideas presented in this chapter about division and hospitality. Use the scale below each statement to assess how much you agree with it, choosing one answer for each row. Then begin some leadership conversations by comparing how much your responses align with the outlook of others in your church. There is space at the bottom of each list item for you to jot down any thoughts or ideas.

1. **The number of people who *leave* our church as "church refugees" is on the rise.**

☐	☐	☐	☐	☐
STRONGLY DISAGREE	DISAGREE	UNCERTAIN OR NO OPINION	AGREE	STRONGLY AGREE

2. **The number of "church refugees" who *come* to our church, frustrated by conflict at their former church, is on the increase.**

☐	☐	☐	☐	☐
STRONGLY DISAGREE	DISAGREE	UNCERTAIN OR NO OPINION	AGREE	STRONGLY AGREE

3. **The younger the churchgoer, the weaker his or her skills are at resolving conflict within the church.**

☐	☐	☐	☐	☐
STRONGLY DISAGREE	DISAGREE	UNCERTAIN OR NO OPINION	AGREE	STRONGLY AGREE

4. Reflecting the "Big Sort," many of our attenders don't want to worship, work, or fellowship with those who don't look or act like them.

☐ STRONGLY DISAGREE ☐ DISAGREE ☐ UNCERTAIN OR NO OPINION ☐ AGREE ☐ STRONGLY AGREE

5. We need to work on ways to build a firmer sense of staying power across our church.

☐ STRONGLY DISAGREE ☐ DISAGREE ☐ UNCERTAIN OR NO OPINION ☐ AGREE ☐ STRONGLY AGREE

6. A stronger culture of hospitality will help our church develop a deeper sense of unity.

☐ STRONGLY DISAGREE ☐ DISAGREE ☐ UNCERTAIN OR NO OPINION ☐ AGREE ☐ STRONGLY AGREE

7. Homogeneity may be easier in the short run, but it develops intolerance in the long run.

☐ STRONGLY DISAGREE ☐ DISAGREE ☐ UNCERTAIN OR NO OPINION ☐ AGREE ☐ STRONGLY AGREE

CHAPTER 6

From Silence to Righteousness

WHY RISING GENERATIONS VIEW THEIR FAITH THROUGH THE LENS OF JUSTICE

Dated question: Should our weekend sermon or pulpit prayers specifically mention the justice issue that's been so much in the news this week?

Better question: Where does our church need to become more specific in applying a grander and more transcendent vision for biblical justice?

THE TREND: Doing justice not by reacting to every instance of outrage but by owning the urgent issues in your local community.

Shift #5: *In the past, younger churchgoing generations may have raised few questions about the level of emphasis that their church placed on the intersection between the gospel and contemporary justice issues. However, more recent generations are increasingly skeptical toward institutions—including the church—that are silent on issues of injustice and expect these issues to be addressed practically and systemically. Going forward, church leaders will* *need to read Scripture with a heightened awareness that rising generations are eager to apply the implications of the gospel that speak to social justice.*

Do you know how twenty-year-olds in your community—either churched or unchurched—think and feel about the following issues?

- the killings of George Floyd, Breonna Taylor, and Ahmaud Arbery
- migrant family separations at the southern U.S. border
- school shootings in Parkland, Florida, and Uvalde, Texas
- abuse scandals in various churches and denominations
- disparities in home ownership, wealth, and healthcare affordability based on race
- the impact of climate change on developing nations

The last members of Gen Z (born between 1997–2012) entered grade school as headlines about these issues began dominating the news—along with social media feeds. While they didn't necessarily react by gravitating toward justice and activism, many of them became more socially conscious at their age than previous generations. This situation also created a higher expectation for organizations and institutions to be socially conscious and to respond appropriately in the face of injustice.

Isn't Gen X (born between 1965–1980) anti-institutional, too? Aren't millennials (born between 1981–1997) supposed to be the social justice generation, as Figure 6.1 illustrates? Then how is Gen Z different?

There's a clear progression: Gen Z was raised and mentored by previous generations who made activism normal and passivity shameful. The utopian picture painted for Gen Z (whether accurate or not) and the language provided to them by previous generations (whether biblical or not) has normalized angst and even rage toward societal ills. Moreover, these factors have created a culture of shame—for better or for worse—for those who choose not to engage.

Figure 6.1—Gen Z and Millennials Care Deeply about Social Justice Issues

1. Mental health help / care
2. Racism
3. Poverty / homelessness / hunger
4. Abortion / birth control
5. The economy
6. Gun violence / gun control
7. Animal rights
8. Sexual harassment / abuse
9. Gender equality / sexism
10. Education

YPulse Charity and Activism Survey of 13- to 39-year-olds, January 2023; image courtesy ECFA.

In his book *Fight: How Gen Z Is Channeling Their Fear and Passion to Save America*, John Della Volpe, director of polling at the Harvard Kennedy School Institute of Politics, explains that members of Gen Z are not only more politically engaged than previous generations at their age, but they now live in a world where they expect that the president of the United States can be a Black man and the vice president can be a biracial Black and Asian American woman. This expectation is nearly the opposite of the generation raised in America in 1950 and perhaps even of the generation in 1980. Additionally, while millions of Americans are seemingly doing well socioeconomically, members of Gen Z are well aware of the tens of millions who are not prospering, and they feel obligated to correct this fault. Della Volpe writes about this awareness in his book:

> [A]s a consequence of an unfolding climate crisis, economic upheaval, gun violence, civil unrest, and increasingly brazen displays of intolerance, white nationalism, and hate, Zoomers [his term for Gen Z] have endured more adversity than any generation of young Americans in at

least seventy years. And they know it. The failure of older generations to resolve these challenges weighs heavy on them. For them, America at times has resembled a dystopia. But they won't sit back and take it. They've decided to fight their own war against injustice and inequality right here at home. They can be this century's "Greatest Generation." Every day, they are fighting for America's future. And they're already winning, causing a sea change in politics, the economy, society, and the ways we live, love, and work.[1]

Gen Z is certainly not the *only* hope for the future of the church in North America, but there is no question that this is the generation that will lead it in the decades to come. As they lead congregations, members of Gen Z have a strong sense of awareness that not only should churches address injustices in society according to the Bible, but also that churches will occasionally need to be confronted for their complacency and complicity.

Coming to Grips with Facts and History to Practice Righteousness

Let us consider issues of climate change and environmental justice. Gen Z has become the most vocal and proactive generation concerning stewardship of the planet.[2] However, for various reasons, this issue is hardly front of mind for many American Christians and church leaders. A study by Pew Research Center reflects this dilemma, showing that evangelicals are the least likely group to believe that global climate change is a problem (34 percent compared to 57 percent of all Americans and 70 percent of "religious 'nones'") and that humans are contributing to global warming (32 percent compared to 53 percent of all Americans and 66 percent of "religious 'nones'").[3]

Many older generations—including non-Christians as well as Christians—are still struggling to see the connection between our consumption habits and the expansion of multinational corporations, the depletion of the earth's resources (for example, deforestation), and the human contribution to catastrophes and famines in many regions of the world. Indeed, this long and documented history[4] has been hidden from some of them. Yet global movements such as the Lausanne Movement and Bread for the World are now reminding us that Christians from around the world are increasing their engagement in climate care and justice,[5] especially in parts of the world most affected by climate change. Today's church leaders can see this as a great opportunity to learn and partner with members of the next generation to be a part of healing God's physical creation.

Certainly, we don't necessarily have to make climate justice the top priority of every local church in order to attract more Gen Zers to their fellowship. But, generally speaking, church leaders today should consider growing in knowledge on issues that gravely impact people, so that they can better partner with the next generation in leading the world toward real solutions for what they identify as the most important issues of the future. If we value building a more just society for the future, our learning will include grappling with the facts already in front of us, as well as with the history behind us.

In *The Evangelical Imagination: How Stories, Images, and Metaphors Created a Culture in Crisis*, Karen Swallow Prior considers the history, metaphors, motifs, and pop culture that shaped both the identities and crises American Christians—particularly evangelicals—are facing. She charges:

> The crisis facing American evangelicalism today—manifest in increasing division, decreasing church membership and attendance, mounting revelations of abuse and cover-up of abuse, and an ongoing reckoning with our racist past and present—is one in which the decorative layers that have long adorned the evangelical house are being peeled away. Now we can see, some of us for the first time, the foundational parts of its structure. Some of these parts are solid. Some are rotten. Some can be salvaged. Some ought not to be saved.[6]

Prior takes prominent themes from the evangelical movement such as the Great Awakenings, conversion, testimony, empire, and rapture, and articulates how these often became metaphors and imagery that historically developed both the minds of individual Christians and the character of a broader movement. History unfolds evangelicalism today as something capable of changing the world in positive and healing ways while simultaneously tearing apart parts of society. For many, learning the history of our traditions will force us to confront long-standing structures that have been complicit with the ongoing injustices in our time.

Jemar Tisby, professor of history at Simmons College of Kentucky, exhorts Christians in his book *How to Fight Racism: Courageous Christianity and the Journey toward Racial Justice* that we should study history not just to know about the past but also to know more about ourselves.[7] He outlines some practices that he believes will combat racial injustice as well as other kinds of injustices:

- learn from academic historians how to spot trustworthy history
- learn your local history
- take [monuments of injustices] down
- conduct oral history
- conduct institutional history
- commemorate Juneteenth

All of this is a part of what Tisby refers to as *ad fontes*, or going back to the sources of history for yourself rather than merely relying on censored narratives or, worse, the political spin of cable news networks. In a twenty-first century reality, it is responsible and healthy for a church leader to relearn the history of the world, America, their local community, their own Christian tradition, and overall church history in order to better understand how the church's collective and social consciousness developed. Also, a church that cultivates an understanding of well-documented injustices in its community is more likely to develop a culture of discipleship that is ready to respond when the community is struck with grief and pain.

From "Justice" to "Righteousness"

In our current age of social media, we might be "darned if we do" or "darned if we don't" if we post a statement about any one particular issue that emerges in the cultural purview. It's becoming increasingly difficult for churches and church leaders to avoid "practicing your righteousness before other people in order to be seen" (Matt. 6:1). Most of us don't mean to boast or virtue signal (attempting to show people you're a good person by expressing an opinion acceptable to them) when we post online about a good deed or issue a statement in solidarity with a group that's hurting and feeling unseen. Before the killing of George Floyd, many contemporary pastors would have never expected to endure an extended season of both internal and external criticism for agreeing with the sentiment of something like #BlackLivesMatter.

A pastor we'll call "Richard" was leading a multiracial church when Floyd was killed and sections of America responded by taking to the streets in protest and demonstration. Like many other Christian leaders, Richard felt conflicted about what would be an appropriate response not only as an individual Christian but also as the lead pastor of his church. While the church belonged to a largely white evangelical denomination, almost half the congregation were people of color. Many of Richard's church members were distraught by the killing of Floyd and thought the church needed to speak out in some way. Richard also felt similarly, and after he had a series of meetings with the elder board, the church posted a statement on its social media that included the hashtag #BlackLivesMatter.

Before too long, a group of members criticized and opposed the church leadership's response because they vehemently disagreed with the founders and leaders of the Black Lives Matter organization (BLM). While Richard also did not agree with the stated values of BLM, he felt strongly about standing in solidarity with those most distraught by Floyd's murder, particularly the Black members of their church. He and the elders believed that using the #BlackLivesMatter hashtag was less about BLM and more about the African Americans in their community. The leadership held a meeting for church members to voice their concerns. Sadly, like with many other churches during the COVID-19 pandemic, the convergence of multiple tensions eventually tore a large rift in the congregation. Many people left the church.

When Jesus talked about seeking righteousness (see the discussion just ahead), was he referring to the kind of response Richard and the elders gave after the killing of Floyd? Was their response ultimately just virtue signaling or giving in to what some identify as a Marxist organization and a left-wing agenda? Was Richard only a social justice weekend warrior and an opportunist using Floyd's name? Or was the collective and social consciousness of the church so undeveloped that its members could not understand the long and complex history of biased policing in Black communities that imposed a heavy toll, including deaths?

When societal tensions are high and pressure is mounting to make a public statement on a justice issue, church leaders do well to take the time to understand the array of perspectives held among church membership before answering public callouts. Processing the internal postures that church members have toward one another is just as important as posting an external stance that church leaders have on an issue, if not more.

Many churches and church leaders did not have high enough levels of internal understanding and harmony needed to deal with a specific response to Floyd's death (or to other examples of a similar nature). When any kind of congregational demand was placed on them through engagement of the issue, their wells were not deep enough to sustain a long-term response.

Churches must cultivate righteousness from the inside in order to contend for justice on the outside.

Herein lies the issue that young leaders need consistently modeled for them before they begin leading for the future: churches must cultivate righteousness from the inside in order to contend for justice on the outside.

In the New Testament, justice and righteousness are intertwined. Likewise, faith that fails to cultivate biblical righteousness will not contend for biblical justice.

In Matthew 5:6, Jesus declares, "Blessed are those who hunger and thirst for righteousness, for they shall be satisfied." The Greek word *dikaiosynēn* (δικαιοσύνην), translated here as "righteousness," can also be translated as "justice." In its most foundational sense, *dikaiosynēn* implies a balanced society. Plato develops and imagines the ancient Greek idea of *dikaiosynēn* in *The Republic*, understanding it to be a harmony of the individual person doing what is right in a way that balances society and leads to flourishing without inflicting injustice upon others. Whether Jesus was alluding to this Greek concept is hard to discern, but a fuller meaning of justice and righteousness is certainly embedded in the New Testament's elaboration of Jesus's words in Matthew 5:6. Scripture links the harmony of society to the well-being of the individual, always having others in mind.

Jesus says to his first followers that they are blessed when they hunger and thirst for that vision of justice and righteousness. In fact, the desire for this vision is a sort of self-fulling prophecy: if you want it, you are filled by it. But this isn't an attainable goal on our own. Attaining righteousness always requires an expense, and the gospel reminds us that God pays this expense. Jesus wanted his disciples to desire something that only God could fulfill. So, to hunger and thirst for this vision is to want God to show up and achieve justice. More simply, it means just wanting God.

Virtue signaling is ultimately hollow; it is neither effective nor real. Trendy justice is shallow because it always imposes a cost on someone else and is mainly about balancing and reappropriating power. Those on either side of critical race theory (CRT) likely realize that a group of people gain power only when another loses it.

However, Jesus throughout his ministry teases out a grander vision for the church to begin living out kingdom righteousness as a microcosm for the world to witness (Matt. 5:13–16): You must cultivate righteousness from the inside in order to contend for justice on the outside. You must cultivate God's character because God is a God of righteousness and justice (Deut. 32:4; Psalm 11:7; Isa. 30:18). Consequently, we are to "seek first the kingdom of God and his righteousness" (Matt. 6:33).

This pursuit of God's kingdom and righteousness reflects a deeper understanding of justice that will outlast trendy notions—and, as history will prove, it will outlast even our modern civic and political notions. Jesus's vision for righteousness is just what young people need to not become skeptics after burning out as activists. Their chants of "No justice, no peace!" are spot on, but they cannot achieve justice and peace by their own power. The church of the future can learn to be present with such people today amid their activism so it can refuel them with a grander and more transcendent Scripture-based vision for justice. Midtown Church offers tremendous insight and inspiration for congregations who desire to make biblical justice a prominent value.

> **Jesus's vision for righteousness is just what young people need to not become skeptics after burning out as activists.**

Midtown Church

SACRAMENTO CONGREGATION PURSUES JUSTICE FROM SERMONS TO COMMUNITY SERVICE

At Midtown Church in downtown Sacramento, the need for justice is evident just outside its building. "The displaced community is not hard to see—it is literally on the front steps and on our sidewalk," said Susie Gamez, co-lead senior pastor of the multiethnic congregation located a block from Interstate 80 in California's capital city. "When you're exiting the freeway, it's everywhere."

As the region's homeless population has surged in recent years, the church has partnered with other congregations to help their unhoused neighbors. "We do sack lunches and we'll bring them down to the different communities—but we'll also collect laundry, wash it for them, and return it back," Gamez said.

Whether in service, sermons, or the mere presence of the diverse team at its helm—Gamez co-leads with Bob Balian, an Armenian man who founded the church in 2011, and Efrem Smith, a Black man known for his nationwide work on racial justice issues—Midtown aims to live out its mission of developing "Cross-Cultural, Reconciling and Justice-Oriented Disciple Makers."

Gamez, 45, a self-described "Korean girl from Canada" who is married to a Mexican man, joined the staff as a teaching pastor in 2021 after working for a missions organization and living on a block of south central Los Angeles, where residents represented dozens of countries. Arriving at Midtown, she found a "refreshing" approach to diversity. "Oftentimes, even if you have a multiethnic church there's still a great degree of white centering that happens," she said, describing other congregations where discussions of race were reserved solely for Black History Month. "Even the way in which we talk about justice or reconciliation or diversity, it's not like we have a series in February or we have a guest preacher come in and talk about it. It really is woven into the DNA of who we are."

In fact, Midtown had once been one campus of a larger church. However, after Balian, Midtown's founding pastor and a chaplain of the Sacramento Kings NBA basketball team, spoke alongside the team in support of its 2020 Black Lives Matter protest, a rift over how to address racial matters led Midtown to become a separate congregation. It now has a weekly attendance of 3,500 to 4,000 people worshiping on two campuses: the downtown location and the Elk Grove campus.

"While there is an intentionality about representing diversity," Gamez commented, "it's not just like a surface-level diversity." Indeed, the intergenerational church has a congregation that is about 35 percent

African American and 35 percent white, with Latino, Asian, and mixed-race families comprising about 30 percent of the worshipers.

Gamez also noted, "During our time of offerings, we often say, 'You don't give to Midtown; you give through Midtown.'" One of the recipients of these offerings is an elementary school two miles away whose student population is in the community's lowest socioeconomic level. "We found out that their field trips were all going to get canceled because they couldn't pay for them and they didn't have transportation for the kids," Gamez recalled. "So we funded the field trips, [and] got all the transportation for them." Staffers and congregants also helped renovate the school's teacher's lounge, stocking it with snacks and supplies.

Midtown also aids its own members by keeping gift cards on hand if they need assistance in purchasing their week's groceries.

On the other end of the economic scale, the church includes leaders like NFL player Arik Armstead, whose mother is a care pastor at the church. "He's also very much remembering the community that surrounds us, and so he's got the Armstead Academic Project, whose main goal is to help equalize educational opportunities," remarked Gamez.

Smith is the board president of Sacramento Area Congregations Together, which pushed back after antisemitic language was uttered at city council meetings and urged city authorities to halt the towing of vehicles that had become homeless shelters. In addition, Pastor Tyronne Gross, the campus pastor at Midtown's Elk Grove campus, founded the Table Community Foundation, which offers after-school programs, mentoring opportunities, and sports activities to area students. Finally, Pastor Gil Acevedo, Midtown's youth ministry director, runs a micro business selling T-shirts to help support anti-trafficking causes through his Modern Abolition nonprofit.

"It's just not uncommon for us to have something outside of the church that is somehow also connected to the church yet is broader than just Midtown," said Gamez, who has advocated for TearFund, a Christian charity that seeks the end of global poverty. "I still do a lot of outside speaking, and oftentimes I'm asked to speak on matters of racial justice or diversity."

For Gamez, just being herself is an act of justice. "I say this to some of my friends, too, especially those who are women of color, when they say, 'Do I have to have five messages in my back pocket to speak about racial justice?' Even the fact that you are a woman of color who is filling the pulpit is an act of resistance to some. But it's an act of worship. It's an act of hope. It's an act of faith. So if you know that you're called to it, be faithful to it," she explained.

That doesn't mean everyone agrees with Gamez when she preaches a warning that being complacent about injustice can lead to being complicit in social evils.[8] "If you've been at the church for more than a year, these things that we say in our sermons shouldn't be surprising to you," she said. "But it's also encouraging because there are people who are on the journey and recognize, 'Hey, this is new for me.' There are also definitely people who are more on the conservative side of things who would say, 'Hey, that really challenged me.'"

In Gamez's sermons, she can naturally speak about the people who may often be ignored. Likewise, the church's members typically have a book club reading about welcoming the foreigner; attend a racial reconciliation group studying a faith-based diversity, equity, and inclusion curriculum; or regularly wash the laundry of unhoused people.

In June 2023, Gamez first acknowledged people who might normally be overlooked—the person who set up her lectern, the ushers, and the people watching online—before she turned to her text in Genesis about the maidservant Hagar. "Jesus had a lens to see people who are on the margins, and that [fact] actually often comes out in my preaching," she said. "We have an opportunity to center people who aren't usually centered or bring people into the fold to help them feel like they belong—and that's living out the gospel."

Ancient and Modern Peacemaking

The vision for justice is older than the New Testament and the ancient Greek world. Seeking righteousness and pursuing justice are activities within the subset of a host of other human activities that are part of establishing *shalom*.

When people march in protest of an injustice, they often chant, "No justice, no peace!" However, it is potentially more profound of a statement from a biblical perspective when the church lives out the Old Testament sentiment of "No *shalom*, no justice!"

Shalom is no small concept in the Bible. Outside the person of God, it is a grand idea that keeps the biblical narrative moving forward optimistically throughout the Old Testament after the fall in Genesis 3. *Shalom* is also the ancient idea that the world and everything in it will be at peace, the human race will flourish, and the earth will be governed with goodness. It is what God told his covenant people exiled in Babylon to seek—not just for their home city of Jerusalem (City of *Shalom*), but for the foreign land in which they now lived. Their task as his people in exile was to put down roots and to have a posture of prayer and action toward even the Babylonian cities becoming cities of *shalom* (Jer. 29:4–7).

Perhaps like no other period in our lifetime, church leaders need to teach Christians what it means to wear new "shoes for your feet, having put on the readiness given by the gospel of *peace*" (Eph. 6:15, emphasis added). Peacemaking amid our age of anxiety is both restorative and preventative when addressing injustice. When church leaders genuinely believe that the gospel humbles the proud and lifts up the lowly, they will gain a crucial ability to disciple and equip church members to be active peacemakers in their community. They will bring *shalom* to every nook, cranny, crack, and crevice of society.

> Peacemaking amid our age of anxiety is both restorative and preventative when addressing injustice.

Amy L. Sherman is the director of the Sagamore Institute's Center on Faith in Communities (CFIC), a capacity-building initiative for churches and community-based organizations. It aims to help leaders invest more effectively and strategically in their communities as they address poverty and injustice.[9] In her book *Agents of Flourishing: Pursuing Shalom in Every Corner of Society*, Sherman outlines principles and practical steps for churches to take toward pursuing peace in local communities. She also offers a multitude of stories about churches and Christian organizations learning how to practice restorative justice. They are putting righteousness into action based on 1) relational and holistic ministry, 2) asset-based approaches, and 3) stewarding power faithfully. But, to Sherman, the language of peacemaking unlocks the imagination for how the local church can see itself: it is not standing on the outside of injustice, but—as an exilic community—is in need of reconciliation yet is simultaneously an agent for reconciliation.

The theme of flourishing provides a comprehensive long-term perspective for Christians and churches to incarnate the gospel so it can bring peace into their communities for multiple generations. This theme is both restorative and preventative, and it assumes the dignity and value of both those serving and those being served because the *shalom* model achieves justice through co-creative means. Each party thus gains, and never at the expense of the other.

Correcting the Most Urgent Issue in Your Community

The church of the future should be the people and the place where the community runs to for advocacy and support when instability happens. For example, prior to the COVID-19 pandemic the United States had a fairly welcoming process for asylum seekers to establish their case for border entry. But because of the pandemic and the large number of migrants coming to the borders claiming asylum, Title 42 was put in place as a governmental policy that allowed U.S. Border Patrol agents to quickly turn asylum seekers away at the border before being granted entry. At the end of 2022, Title 42 expired and tens of thousands of migrants claiming asylum flooded the borders. After the Border Patrol processed the migrants and granted them entry into the U.S., many of the Southern border states flew or bussed them into Northern cities that had declared themselves open to any migrant who could get there. By the summer of 2023, Chicago had received thousands of asylum seekers, mostly from Venezuela, with upward of eight hundred people sleeping in police stations because of the expedited bussing and lack of adequate housing in the city.

Jorge Rodriquez, pastor of Grace Family Church, a congregation started in 2019 in the Rogers Park neighborhood of Chicago, had developed a good relationship with the civic leaders of the community. As asylum seekers arrived at the nearby police precinct, the captain immediately reached out to Rodriquez for help. Because Grace Family Church had instinctively done much of what Amy Sherman outlines in *Agents of Flourishing*, and even more so because Rodriquez was well-acquainted with the stories and reasons for why the asylum seekers were arriving, its members were ready from the moment they received the precinct's invitation. Rodriquez posted photos of the precinct and of asylum seekers receiving services on Facebook, but was careful not to show any faces. His caption read:

> SO PROUD of the way the folks at Grace Family Church have stepped up to serve and minister this week!!! They are working at the police department bringing food, blankets, sharing scripture and praying with our migrants. Keep them, and other Hispanic and non-Hispanic churches in prayer as today 🙏!

> TAN ORGULLOSO en como los hermanos/nas de la iglesia han tomado el reto de servir y ministrar esta semana!!! Trabajando en la estación de policía ministrando con comida, sábanas, compartiendo las escrituras y orando con nuestros inmigrantes. Manténganlos hoy a ellos, y a otras iglesias hispanas y no hispanas, en oración 🙏![10]

The post had no viral likes, comments, or shares. It was just a simple message letting Rodriquez's social network know what the church was doing. None of his friends would confuse his post as virtue signaling, because what he did was neither a hollow nor a shallow act. Rodriguez and Grace Family Church are fully engaged in their community, and they were invited into something by the community that was urgent, restorative, and perhaps even preventative. They saw this opportunity as an honor and a responsibility to bring *shalom* and justice into their corner of the city.

That's the kind of church whose approach to biblical justice will cause rising generations to take note, get involved, and be drawn to the Prince of Peace whom it represents.

One Degree of Change

Next are simple statements adapted from various ideas presented in this chapter about justice and righteousness. Use the scale below each statement to assess how much you agree with it, choosing one answer for each row. Then begin some leadership conversations by comparing how much your responses align with the outlook of others in your church. There is space at the bottom of each list item for you to jot down any thoughts or ideas.

1. **Gen Z is leading the way with a strong awareness that churches should address injustices in society according to the Bible.**

☐	☐	☐	☐	☐
STRONGLY DISAGREE	DISAGREE	UNCERTAIN OR NO OPINION	AGREE	STRONGLY AGREE

2. Our church has much to learn so it can better apply the New Testament's teaching about justice.

☐	☐	☐	☐	☐
STRONGLY DISAGREE	DISAGREE	UNCERTAIN OR NO OPINION	AGREE	STRONGLY AGREE

3. The church of the future should be the people and the place that the community runs to for advocacy and support when instability happens.

☐	☐	☐	☐	☐
STRONGLY DISAGREE	DISAGREE	UNCERTAIN OR NO OPINION	AGREE	STRONGLY AGREE

4. The church can learn to be present with younger generations today amid their activism so that it can refuel them with a grander and more transcendent vision for justice.

☐	☐	☐	☐	☐
STRONGLY DISAGREE	DISAGREE	UNCERTAIN OR NO OPINION	AGREE	STRONGLY AGREE

5. Biblical peacemaking in today's age of anxiety is both restorative and preventative when addressing injustice.

☐	☐	☐	☐	☐
STRONGLY DISAGREE	DISAGREE	UNCERTAIN OR NO OPINION	AGREE	STRONGLY AGREE

CHAPTER 7

From Racial Tension to Community Blessing

WHY CHURCHES NEED DIVERSITY BEYOND TOKENISM

Dated question: How can we help minorities feel more included in our church?

Better question: How can our church push the boundaries of what it means to be ethnically inclusive and diverse?

THE TREND: Creating multiethnicity not by managing diversity but by blessing all people groups in your community through the gospel.

Shift #6: *In the past, most churches were of one predominant race or ethnicity, and few churchgoers directly challenged that social norm. Currently, a heightened awareness of racial diversity has led to more diverse congregations, with younger generations feeling that something must be wrong if a congregation is not intentionally diverse. Going forward, the role of race and ethnicity*

*will become strongly linked to how God will use the gospel to bless
every "tribe and language and people and nation" (Rev. 5:9).*

On several occasions, Martin Luther King Jr. famously said that eleven
o'clock on Sunday morning was "the most segregated hour in America."
The book *Divided by Faith*, published in 2000 by Michael O. Emerson
and Christian Smith, was the result of a large research project seeking
to understand how churches were making progress in the conversation around race, ethnicity, and diversity in churches across America.
Emerson, now a fellow at Rice University's Baker Institute for Public
Policy, conducted the main research for this book. In an interview with
one of us authors, Emerson candidly admitted that "I literally felt sick in
my stomach" after he had combed through all the data, which included
telephone surveys of 2,000 people and 200 face-to-face interviews. At the
start of the twenty-first century, and more than a generation since the
Civil Rights Act of 1964, Emerson's data affirmed that Martin Luther
King Jr.'s observation still held true.

Prior to the year 2000, some churches scattered across the nation
were intentionally seeking racial and ethnic diversity among their membership. However, *Divided by Faith* became the justification and the
fuel that sparked what has now become a movement for multiethnic
churches. Since then, many books, conferences, and research projects
have been devoted to proliferating intentional diversity in churches.
Twenty years later, nearly a quarter of churches in America were considered racially diverse, meaning at least 20 percent of the congregation was
of a race different from the majority race.[1]

But what does diversity *truly* mean? Can it be meaningfully measured by percentages and quotas? And what are multiethnic churches
really achieving, anyway?

Korie Little Edwards is a leading scholar of race and religion at Ohio
State University, focusing her research on interracial and multiethnic
churches.[2] In her 2021 Chr*istianity Today* article "The Multiethnic Church

Movement Hasn't Lived Up to Its Promise," Edwards points out that even if a church has a racially diverse membership, the church's leadership may still reflect the majority racial group. Thus, the majority defines much of the culture of the church and the minority has no real influence or authority in the church.[3] While much of Edwards's article focuses on the unique history and dynamics between Blacks and whites in

> **Diversity is meaningful only if there is true belonging and equity for those in the minority.**

America, the same dynamics hold true in other kinds of interracial or multiethnic congregations: diversity is meaningful only if there is true belonging and equity for those in the minority.

While belonging has always been a component of diversity, church leaders are increasingly becoming aware that diversity in itself is not a lofty enough goal, especially when it preserves a majority-dominance mentality. Meanwhile, the United States has diversified at a rapid rate, especially since the late 1970s and early 1980s. To provide context, this was the racial composition of America back in 1980 (when Rick and Kay Warren started Saddleback Church):[4]

- 80%—White
- 11.5%—Black
- 6.5%—Latino/Hispanic
- 1.8%—Asian
- 0.2%—Other

Compare this to the latest U.S. Census data, which shows the racial composition of America to currently be the following:[5]

- 57.8%—White
- 18.7%—Latino/Hispanic
- 12.1%—Black
- 6%—Asian
- 5.4%—Other

The U.S. Census projects that by 2045, America will have no majority race. Whites will, for the first time, make up less than half of the nation's population.[6]

The dramatic increase of minorities in America, especially among Latino/Hispanic, Asian, and multiracial populations, has shifted much of the conversation away from using just a Black–white framework for dialogue toward constructing a more complex and sophisticated paradigm for the future of organizations, particularly churches. Meaningful diversity for the future isn't just about seeing majority-minority dynamics. Rather, it is about recognizing how to achieve unity through distributing representation and authority without marginalizing any existing groups, and especially not prioritizing and pitting one racial group over and against the others.

Figure 7.1—America's Rapidly Changing Racial Profile

	White	Hispanic	Black	Asian	Native	Two or more races
Year	General Population					
1950	88%	2%	10%	<1	<1	**
2000	69%	13%	12%	4%	1%	1%
2050	44%	27%	14%	8%	1%	6%
	Protestant Churchgoers					
2020	77%	5%	10%	2%	2%	4%

Population data and projections from U.S. Census Bureau; church data from Hartford Institute for Religion Research; image courtesy ECFA.

Demographics and the People of God

While it's useful to unpack what demographers and sociologists of religion have to say about the future of the church in America, church leaders must continuously evaluate how the biblical narrative has accounted for demographics and diversity in the formation of the people of God. Spiritual insights into our modern notions of race are present as early as the book of Genesis and remain a factor all the way through the Bible to its final book, Revelation.

While there are more options, we have chosen two familiar yet key points in the Bible that have bookended how people of God understood demography and diversity and sought to integrate them into the life and mission of the church. And while it's important not to read modern notions of race, ethnicity, and diversity into the biblical narratives, it is valuable to examine the following passages in light of how the present church is navigating the social constructs of our day.

The Call of Abraham in Genesis

In Genesis 12, God calls Abraham (then known as Abram) out of his father's land and promises him three things (vv. 2–3):

1. I will make of you a great nation.
2. I will bless you and make your name great, so that you will be a blessing.
3. I will bless those who bless you, and him who dishonors you I will curse, and in you all the families of the earth will be blessed.

What has been called the Abrahamic Covenant is one of the earliest revelations of how God would create for himself a nation or people—*goy* (גּוֹי) in the Hebrew. This new nation would exist in contrast to the other nations surrounding Abraham. Later, in sections such as Deuteronomy 4, the newly forming people of God came to realize that God had intentionally set them apart, juxtaposing them with already existing nations. Thus, God was purposeful in creating distinctions between people groups for his redemptive purpose.

It is worth noting that in the blessing of Genesis 12, "nation" or "people" is more of an ethnic-linguo category than a geopolitical identifier. It is certainly not the same as the nation-state divisions that make up our world map today. However, while the designations are dissimilar, they are also not mutually exclusive. We see here that, starting with Abraham, God was creating a specific people for himself. In doing so, God affirmed the process of ethnogenesis, in which a group of people become ethnically distinct from others.

The rest of the Genesis text, and arguably the rest of the Old Testament, is the unfolding of this promise from God to Abraham—the development of a unique nation. Abraham, who could not be considered a Hebrew or a Jew in his own time, would be called out by God to begin a nation that had the expressed purpose of blessing all other nations in the world. And while this nation would eventually become a geopolitical nation-state called Israel, the people of God have always been part of pushing the boundaries of what it means to be ethnically inclusive and diverse.[7] Given how comparatively small the earth's population would have been at that time (possibly estimated to be as low as twenty-seven million people[8]), the original people of God could have grown in size and influence only as they navigated the diversity of the known world at the time.

> The people of God have always been part of pushing the boundaries of what it means to be ethnically inclusive.

In short, the process of coming out of one's own heritage to be used by God to make a new people that blesses other surrounding groups is a pattern we see throughout the Scriptures as we consider the growth of the people of God. The destiny of God's people in Abraham's day, as well as throughout history, was driven by their becoming a blessing to the global demography.

The Vision of a New Song in Revelation

For some, the application for Revelation 5:9–10 in our modern day looks like a large worship sanctuary reflecting an ethnically diverse congregation singing songs of praise and adoration to Jesus. And, perhaps for a time, this view has given some basic justification for the intentional development of racially and ethnically diverse congregations. However, by itself, Revelation 5 does not give an imperative for local church diversity, and it does not support the idea that the church in its ultimate form will look like a multiethnic congregation.

The vision given to the Apostle John evoked a feeling of desperation and sadness in him (v. 3–4). No one in heaven or on earth was capable of opening the scroll that contained the oracles of God for the destiny of the world. John had a sinking feeling that due to all that had transpired in the world from the beginning until now, no one was able or worthy of projecting a hopeful future for the world. Thankfully, John then received the news that Jesus, who fulfilled the prophecies of the Old Testament given to the people of God, was worthy to open the scroll to announce the future of the world.

John then witnesses an overwhelming and jubilant eruption of heavenly creatures and those called the twenty-four elders who understood and felt the magnitude of Jesus's worthiness. They viscerally reacted to the existential reality that Jesus was God incarnate who fulfilled the narratives of the Old Testament patriarchs, such as what had been promised to Abraham. See verses 9 and 10:

And they sang a new song, saying,

> "Worthy are you to take the scroll
>> and to open its seals,
> for you were slain, and by your blood you ransomed
>> people for God
>> from every tribe and language and people and
>>> nation,
> and you have made them a kingdom and priests to
>> our God,
>> and they shall reign on the earth."

The singers of this song were confronted with the reality that in Jesus every nation would have redeemed people among its inhabitants who would usher in God's kingdom in their cultural context, representing his just rule and reign on earth. A passage that we are at times tempted to reduce to a multiethnic worship service is actually meant to inspire hope for global unity and justice.

Revelation 7:9–10 gives us even more clarity on this:

> After this I looked, and behold, a great multitude that no one could number, from every nation, from all tribes and peoples and languages, standing before the throne and before the Lamb, clothed in white robes, with palm branches in their hands, and crying out with a loud voice, "Salvation belongs to our God who sits on the throne, and to the Lamb!"

No one auditorium can contain the global nature of Jesus's redemption. It is worldwide and multiethnic—each unit of people worshipping Jesus from their own locations historically, geographically, and demographically.

To that end, a congregational makeup that fosters a greater understanding of this impending reality may or may not be racially and ethnically diverse. In a complex modern world, a church that is diverse racially, ethnically, and socioeconomically may have a greater likelihood of raising awareness about parts of the world that are without the just rule and reign of Jesus. But awareness can also be found in a marginalized church in Western Europe or in a persecuted church in Iran. A meaningfully diverse church exists to be a voice for the suffering of people around the world, not just for the luxury and privilege of curating an auditorium or staff team.

Tokenism and Managed Diversity

A church that seeks to bless the nations around it and works toward God's just rule and reign on earth must go beyond diversity as percentages and quotas, and it must also resist tokenism. At its core, *tokenism* is the policy or practice of employing someone from a minority group in order to avoid criticism or give the appearance that all people are being treated fairly. While modern usage of this term now spans categories beyond race and ethnicity into gender, sexuality, socioeconomics, and class, the word was not regularly used until the 1960s when Blacks were being integrated into predominantly white spaces. Even then, leaders such as Martin Luther King Jr. were challenging tokenism as impeding true progress in society. King would address it publicly in a 1962 *New York Times* article entitled "The Case against 'Tokenism'" and in his classic book *Why We Can't Wait*, published in 1964.

At its core, racial and ethnic tokenism preserves majority dominance. In a slow-changing society, majority dominance is often the reality of the day. However, in a fast-changing society majority dominance will almost always mean leading from an expiring narrative and paradigm. Those who do not fully understand this dynamic will practice tokenism as a shortcut to diversity, not realizing that it will fail to lead them toward a better future. More often, such people engage in practices of tokenism because they hope to avoid criticism of not having enough diversity or perhaps desire to cover shame left over from previous discriminatory practices.

> At its core, racial and ethnic tokenism preserves majority dominance. In a fast-changing society, such dominance will almost always mean leading from an expiring narrative and paradigm.

While there are noble reasons for a church to diversify its leadership teams and visible staff, the ones who practice tokenism almost never take a deep dive into their history of racial biases and the internal systems and processes that make it nearly impossible to meaningfully and authentically diversify. Without a thorough examination, employing minority leaders or putting minority people in visible places without the hope of creating deep and internal change is essentially a marketing ploy and a form of tokenism.

This phenomenon is sometimes true for the wave of new churches started in the urban core of American cities by parent churches located in the surrounding suburbs. An example comes from an ethnographic study by Jessica M. Barron of an urban congregation in Chicago called Downtown Church. In her book *The Urban Church Imagined: Religion, Race, and Authenticity in the City*, Barron writes:

> *Racial utility* occurs when the racial status of an individual serves the corporate needs of those in authority, in this case, the leadership staff at Downtown Church. In this congregation, the racial utility of members of color is incorporated to symbolize a fabricated diversity, imagined as a necessity for a church located in the city.[9]

Barron sees the utilization of race—specifically the appropriation of Black culture—as a commodity of the church to make it a more appealing option for urbanites who are church seekers. The placement of minority people on the church's website and as greeters and onstage personalities gives the church a perception of being "urban" and "of the city." However, the leadership is dominated and driven by the majority culture of the suburban parent church. Barron would say in this case that church leadership was managing diversity so that middle-class church seekers could consume it as an experience and as a part of a religious identity.[10]

Racial and ethnic tokenism in the church can lead to five potentially detrimental effects:[11]

1. **Hyper-Visibility.** The tokenized person is often more visible than others and called upon to speak on behalf of others. This may cause people to pay more attention to how tokenized people look and behave. This person may feel constantly evaluated and scrutinized, especially in regard to his or her race.
2. **Hyper-Contrast.** The tokenized person is often perceived as different from the majority group. Differences can be highlighted over commonalities, and boundaries between this person and the majority group are unclear and

inauthentic. These boundaries can often lead to isolation and even mistreatment.

3. **Role Encapsulation.** The tokenized person is expected to play a particular role that is usually stereotyped in popular media or imagined by the majority group. The person can also be pigeon-holed and is unable to see vertical movement within church leadership or lateral movement across other kinds of ministries.

4. **Emotional and Spiritual Trauma.** In time, a tokenized person will often feel used and unknown, causing emotional trauma. If church leadership continues to justify how this person is being represented and used in church through Scripture and for ministry growth, spiritual trauma can also eventually develop.

5. **Organizational Stifling.** In the end, tokenism does not change anything since it is only implemented at a superficial level. A church that wants to experience true and authentic diversity will always fall short because tokenism expects the minority population to conform and assimilate, not to offer more of who they are to the church.

Tokenism often goes undetected in the short run. In fact, most churches that practice tokenism have no intentions of doing so. But good intentions without robust conversation and a deep conviction for systemic and culture change are misguided. And while certainly not every church in America needs to be racially diverse and multiethnic, for those that choose to be—and for the contexts and communities that demand it—the pathway beyond tokenism will include church leaders who are capable of handling normative, intelligent, loving, and ever-growing conversations about what it means to practically embrace and appropriately advocate for the minorities among them. The following story illustrates how one church achieved a natural and meaningful diversity through reflecting its already diverse community.

> **Good intentions without robust conversation and a deep conviction for systemic and culture change are misguided.**

Alliance Tabernacle

BROOKLYN CHURCH CHOOSES TO REFLECT
ITS MULTICULTURAL NEIGHBORHOOD

Alliance Tabernacle in the central area of Brooklyn, New York, has lived through neighborhood change after neighborhood change.

The church, currently one of the largest congregations in the Christian and Missionary Alliance denomination, started just over a century ago, birthed at a tent revival in the Crown Heights and Bedford-Stuyvesant area of the New York borough. "Unfortunately, the church was not really receptive to the demographic shifts and changes, and so it moved," said the Rev. Charles O. Galbreath, pastor since 2010.

Moving away from a neighborhood that had become a thriving African American community, the church, having relocated to East Flatbush, had a predominantly Irish and Italian congregation in the 1940s to 1960s, reflecting the community there. Then, by the 1970s, an influx of people from Caribbean islands began to dominate the area. This time, instead of relocating, the church intentionally changed its demographics to match the neighborhood. It continued to do so as the neighborhood changed further over time.

When Galbreath, now 40, became pastor, the congregation was primarily Jamaican. Its membership now represents twenty-six nations, primarily from the Caribbean, in the area of East Flatbush that has been designated "Little Caribbean" and a section of it "Little Haiti."

"We still have people who are coming in from Trinidad and from Guyana," Galbreath said concerning the congregation, which holds two morning services on Sunday and has hundreds in attendance. "But because we've been there for a while, we've also seen their children grow up in the church. We've seen folks get married and have husbands and wives, babies, and all those different things that continue to add to the life of the church."

Although East Flatbush has had an overwhelming Black population (92%), Galbreath said that he felt a call to reach those who comprise the minority in his community. "We're seeing a lot of people moving into Brooklyn, and the demographics shifting and changing . . . particularly due to our white brothers and sisters who are coming into New York City," he remarked. "So, as a result of that, how do we develop a discipleship model that is not just connected to those who are here, but also to those who are coming?"

Over about four years, through what Galbreath admits has been "some trial and error," Alliance Tabernacle has started a new group of worshipers on a separate campus dubbed Mission Church, intentionally planning it to look different from the multicultural, mostly Caribbean church that spawned it. The gathering of dozens of young adults in Gowanus, a neighborhood of coffee shops and art galleries, reflects another type of diversity, comprising a mixed attendance of Latino, white, and Caribbean people.

"I really believe in the multicultural church," said Galbreath, who grew up in Prince George's County, Maryland, in a racially mixed church led by his father for thirty-two years. "But I think the framing of a multicultural church has predominantly been from a majority cultural model, so that it is birthed out of the majority culture, which then influences what an ethnic church may look like in a particular community."

But Galbreath, who did his PhD research on preaching to Black millennials, seeks to reshape that model. "There's certain distinctives and there's a certain ethos in regard to not only worship and justice and community and family that is found within the Black church context, which can help disciple and guide not just Black churches but also multiethnic, multigenerational churches," he explained, outlining his approach to starting a new congregation. "Just because it is birthed from a Black church does not necessarily indicate it is just going to be a Black church, but there's certain ethics that we believe are cross-racial and cross-cultural that can help influence and, I believe, help heal and bring forth the kingdom."

Three ethical principles of the Black church that Galbreath hopes can transfer to other congregations, including Mission Church, are deep roots in scriptural texts, a prophetic voice that speaks against injustice, and "radical fellowship and intentional mentoring of identity," be that Cuban, Dominican, or Iowan.

Mission Church, for which Galbreath's Alliance Tabernacle intentionally chose a Caucasian-Latina pastor, looks different from the church on the main campus, not only because of the size and racial/ethnic description of the congregation but also due to the structure of its space and its worship. Those gathering on the separate campus meet in an industrial loft at a different time. Monthly, the service is in the form of Dinner Church, a movement where attendees share faith and food around a table. With or without a meal, there's more time for dialogue between the Mission Church leader and the worshipers. There is also more openness to questions from those who gather, and the church sends invitations to those who have been estranged from church to visit by hanging out and enjoying a meal.

Galbreath acknowledged that he had to come around to the notion that a different congregation in his church's context needed to be in a separate location. "Instead of getting a whole new space," he originally thought, "we could do it in our location and try to frame it as something different, but it just was not connecting" with the population they were hoping to attract.

After several years, the church relaunched Mission Church in a location where it now has sponsored art shows, music gatherings, and spoken-word performances in addition to worship services.

Galbreath said that he fielded questions from longtime members who've been at the traditional site for decades and can't quite grasp this different congregational model located about four miles away in Gowanus.

"It's alright. It's OK," he responded to them. But he also suggested that they consider people other than themselves who might find the nontraditional campus to be more attractive than the service they attend. "What about your cousin, what about your daughter, what about your niece, who are not necessarily coming to our worship experience because they don't feel comfortable or they don't feel connected?" he asked them.

Galbreath understands their questions, but he's also confident in his explanation that there's more than one way to do church. "I believe God speaks in multiple traditions," he asserted. "We want to see what we can do to facilitate that belief in our various capacities."

Mission Church attendees have joined members of the main campus in protests, including around the death of George Floyd. But they've also committed to local social and justice matters, ranging from aiding a homeless shelter across the street to raising funds for a Peruvian restaurant so that it could remain a central part of their neighborhood.

Galbreath explained that planting churches with different demographics than the original church has long been a part of his denomination's history. "I don't know if we've always done it well, and done it with equity and empowerment," he admitted. "But that's what I want to hope to see—where there is partnership equity in that relationship. And so it's not paternalistic in any type of way, but, rather, it is fully empowering."

Galbreath aims for his main church to guide and influence a new campus but also give it autonomy as it grows. "If you are in a community that is 99 percent Anglo or a community that's 99 percent Asian or a community that's 99 percent Black," he said, "I believe that you're called to a neighborhood. If you serve in that particular neighborhood community context, that's the reality that it's going to be."

Still, Galbreath sees multiethnic congregations as a goal even if they are not an immediate reality: "But if you do see demographic shifts and changes, I believe that this is part of our ethic: to ask, how do we empower, engage, and allow all to be a part of God's kingdom?"

A Better Discourse around Race and Ethnicity

As mentioned earlier, the question of diversity and multiethnicity for church leaders is more of a biblical and theological question than a demographic and sociological question. Demographics and sociology may help us understand *how* America is quickly diversifying, but, in addition to good data science, church leaders must turn to God and the Bible to ask *why* America is quickly diversifying.

At many points, some Christians in America have provided awful and horrific explanations for how races should relate to one another. This is evident in heretical teachings such as the "curse of Ham" (at its worst, God cursed Black people); manifest destiny (at its worst, God authorized the extermination of Native Americans); and, more recently, Kinism[12] (at its worst, God wants various races to live separately). These heresies should not downplay less noticeable but more frequent practices, such as when parents and church leaders use the Bible to justify children not marrying outside of their ethnicity or social class, which are also common among immigrant groups in America.

Asking God about the *why* of diversity isn't primarily about developing a particular theology or social theory for race and ethnicity. It is primarily about a local church working to develop and improve its own discourse around race and ethnicity in its local community so it can appropriately respond to the dynamics that are most within its influence and seek to bless the nations already among its members. In one example, a local Hispanic church experiencing generational transition and seeing an influx of Afghan refugees in its neighborhood will have a nuanced view of diversity in its community. In another instance, a predominantly African American church in a gentrifying neighborhood will ask largely different questions than a pan-Asian church about integrating Asian college students into its congregational life.

Without ignoring national trends and popular literature on race and ethnicity, an authentic discourse on diversity is best developed on the ground and in the immediate community surrounding a church. A local church that understands the bookends of the call of Abraham in Genesis and the vision of a new song in Revelation will be most concerned with blessing the existing people groups around it and bringing God's just rule and reign into its community.

From a church growth perspective, the conversation around race and ethnicity has been in part dedicated to achieving a certain composition of people in Sunday morning worship spaces and eventually a representative body of leaders in boardrooms. This may have been largely due to realizing the limitations of modern church growth theory based on Donald McGavran's "homogeneous unit principle," which postulated that most individuals become Christians in social groups similar to their own.[13] While the topic of diversity is certainly a worthwhile conversation that needs to continue and improve, the larger discourse around this issue in the Bible, from Genesis to Revelation amid both beautiful and tragic stories, has always been about *blessing* and *the kingdom*. This approach inevitably has always encouraged God's people to mobilize and engage others outside of their norm with the love of God.

> An authentic discourse on diversity is best developed on the ground and in the immediate community surrounding a church.

Denise Kimber Buell, professor of religion at Williams College, asserts in her book *Why This New Race: Ethnic Reasoning in Early Christianity* that New Testament Christians were deeply engaged in the process of becoming multiethnic. Thus, their conversion to Jesus was an integral part of navigating their own ethnic identity:

> Ethnic reasoning allowed [early] Christians not only to describe themselves as a people, but also to depict the process of becoming a Christian as one of crossing a boundary from membership in one race to another. . . . Thus what we might conceive of as a religious process, conversion, could be simultaneously imagined as a process of ethnic transformation.[14]

This explanation helps us to understand why members of the church in Antioch were called "Christians" for the first time in Acts 11:26. The conversion of people from disparate nations and manifold personal backgrounds formed something so new that a new social group had to be formed and given a name: Χριστιανούς or *little Christs*. Indeed, members of the early church were all converted to one another in the process of their conversion to Jesus. Those two elements, or two conversions, radically redefined who they were as individuals. Therefore, at the intersection of believers' new lives together, the church in Antioch provided a meaningful model for a unique localized global community.

Models of Racial and Ethnic Diversity

During and after the Jim Crow era in the United States, when state and local statutes had legalized racial segregation, churches and denominations adapted the language of "integration" to describe diversity. Just like a child may have attended a racially integrated school or swam in an integrated community pool, families may have attended a racially integrated congregation. A 1966 article in *Ebony* magazine entitled "Integration: Great Dilemma of the Church: Nation's Foremost Moral Issue Forces Reappraisal of Racially Separate Worship" shows how prominently the term was used to describe churches. The writers give a summons to Christians at the start of a post-Jim Crow America:

> A vacuum now exists in American society. It is essentially a spiritual vacuum. The Supreme Court, the Congress, and the President have swept out legal racial segregation. Only the Churches can fill the empty space with a positive program of brotherhood. *This the Churches must do, whatever the cost.*[15]

The article concludes with a black-and-white photo of Bishop James S. Thomas, a Black Methodist pastor, baptizing a white baby in Monmouth, Iowa. Thomas became one of the first Black bishops to oversee a Methodist Church conference when he was appointed the bishop of the North Central Jurisdiction in 1964.

Since then, the language around diversity has evolved. The most common terms as of late are either *diverse, multicultural, multiracial,* or *multiethnic.* This shift took place partly due to the growth of immigration in the 1970s and 1980s, so that in the 1990s the term *integration*—which was thought more of as a Black–white issue—became obsolete. These replacement terms are accounting for the rise of other visible minority groups that do not participate in the shared struggles of African Americans and that also do not have a long American heritage.

The following chart provides some distinction as to what these terms may mean when used by a church leader. None of the meanings provided are meant to be exhaustive or authoritative, but rather seek to get at the nuances of how people understand social groupings and how churches intentionally aim for diversity.

Many more church types could be added to this chart, specifically those with racial or ethnic identifiers such as "African American Church" or "Indian Church." But the types listed reflect some of the normative terms that try to encompass diversity in churches. Hopefully they can inspire your church to become what the people of God in your community could be.

TERM	MEANING
Diverse Church	has people from various backgrounds and heritages; the broadest term used to describe diversity
Multicultural Church	has people from several distinctly different cultures; the leaders of the church intentionally implement cultural elements from many of the groups into its programming
Multiracial Church	has people from different racial backgrounds; tends to borrow language and concepts from the Black–white discourse
Multiethnic Church	has people from different ethnic groups and nations; usually has a dominant culture to which members tend to conform
Multilingual Church	has people from different language groups; the leaders of the church intentionally integrate different languages into its programming

Multigenerational Church	has people from multiple generations; while most churches are multigenerational, some churches explicitly mention this aspect to set themselves apart from churches that are targeting young adults, young families, or other specific age groups
Immigrant Church	has people who are mostly first-generation immigrants or are led by first-generation immigrant leaders
Second-Generation Church	has people who are mostly second-generation immigrants or are led by second-generation immigrant leaders
Latino/Hispanic Church	has people who speak Spanish or are of Latin American heritage; tends to be first-generation immigrants, with programming held in Spanish, and might include strong second-generation, English-dominant groups
Pan-Asian Church	has people from multiple Asian heritages; programming tends to be in English
"American" Church	a term usually used by immigrant churches to describe predominantly white churches; implies the distance their leaders feel from being native to America
Urban Church	churches located inside the formal limits of a large city with proximity to downtown or densely populated areas; sometimes a euphemism for churches in the inner city or in proximity to Black and brown communities

One Degree of Change⌐

Next are simple statements adapted from various ideas presented in this chapter about race, ethnicity, and diversity. Use the scale below each statement to assess how much you agree with it, choosing one answer for each row. Then begin some leadership conversations by comparing how much your responses align with the outlook of others in your church. There is space at the bottom of each list item for you to jot down any thoughts or ideas.

1. **Scripture has much to say about the importance of God's house as a place of worship for "all the nations" (Mark 11:17, quoting Isaiah 56:7).**

☐	☐	☐	☐	☐
STRONGLY DISAGREE	DISAGREE	UNCERTAIN OR NO OPINION	AGREE	STRONGLY AGREE

2. **It's easy to prioritize one racial group over another unwittingly.**

☐	☐	☐	☐	☐
STRONGLY DISAGREE	DISAGREE	UNCERTAIN OR NO OPINION	AGREE	STRONGLY AGREE

3. **Diversity at church is meaningful only if the minority has true belonging and equity.**

☐	☐	☐	☐	☐
STRONGLY DISAGREE	DISAGREE	UNCERTAIN OR NO OPINION	AGREE	STRONGLY AGREE

4. Meaningful, God-honoring diversity achieves unity through distributing both representation and authority.

☐	☐	☐	☐	☐
STRONGLY DISAGREE	DISAGREE	UNCERTAIN OR NO OPINION	AGREE	STRONGLY AGREE

5. Our church is reaching greater clarity on what models of racial and ethnic diversity it can aim toward for this particular season.

☐	☐	☐	☐	☐
STRONGLY DISAGREE	DISAGREE	UNCERTAIN OR NO OPINION	AGREE	STRONGLY AGREE

6. There are people of certain racial or ethnic groups in my congregation who may have been greeted but are never seriously considered for leadership roles.

☐	☐	☐	☐	☐
STRONGLY DISAGREE	DISAGREE	UNCERTAIN OR NO OPINION	AGREE	STRONGLY AGREE

CHAPTER 8

From Physical Only to
Healthy Hybrid

WHY MORE CHURCH LIFE WILL
HAPPEN VIRTUALLY

Dated question: How do we do in-person church better so that people will want to spend less time online?

Better question: How can we discern God's work everywhere people spend time, especially in the growing digital world?

THE TREND: Embracing technology not by valuing its convenience but by pioneering spaces for Christ to be worshipped and proclaimed.

Shift #7: *In the past Christians tapped technology for helpful one-way broadcasts, from sermons to updates about church happenings. For more recent generations, online technology has allowed various forms of interaction such as chat rooms to discuss sermon applications or hybrid small groups that meet sometimes online and sometimes in person. Going forward, digital technologies will redefine people's perception of "real life,"* *their sense of social identity, and even their primary location for experiencing spiritual outreach and healthy community.*

"Dad, can you give me 10,000 Robux for my birthday?"

Salena was turning six years old and wanted to buy more building tools to finish developing her land in Roblox, a cross-platform online universe that gives people digital real estate to create their own world wherein anyone can virtually visit and interact. The currency of Roblox is Robux, which is currently worth 0.32¢ USD. It isn't cryptocurrency in the true sense of the term, but it is real money to a Robloxian—the race of the human-like sapiens that reside in Roblox and also the term used to refer to someone who plays Roblox.

Until now, Salena has been comfortable inviting only her siblings and cousins to her virtual home. She wants to put finishing touches on it before asking her friends from school and the neighborhood to "come over and play." Salena is not concerned about her physical home being good enough to have friends visit. In fact, many of them do come over. However, her physical house is the home *her parents* are building; Salena's Roblox house, on the other hand, is the home *she* is building. It is bigger and better in some ways than what is in "real life," largely because it reflects how she sees the world. And, besides, eventually every one of Salena's friends can visit whenever he or she pleases, which her parents don't welcome in physical reality!

Roblox is more than just a video game; it is a universe created by young people. Consider how the company describes itself:

> This world is ours for the making. Roblox builds the tools and platform that empower people to create their own immersive experiences, so that any world they can imagine can be brought to life. *Our vision is to reimagine the way people come together to create, play, explore, learn, and connect with one other.*
>
> We don't make Roblox. You do. Roblox is built by a global

community of millions of developers and creators who are always making new experiences for users to explore. Using Roblox tools and technology, *our community is creating new ways for people to connect every day.*[1]

Also, observe Roblox's wide popularity as of 2023:

- Roblox has been downloaded 383 million times.
- Roblox is used by 202 million people every month.
- The number of Roblox daily active users stands at 52.2 million.
- More than 20 million people play Roblox daily.
- 28 percent of daily Roblox users are based in the U.S. and Canada.
- Roblox is played an average of 2.6 hours a day.
- The fastest-growing age demographic on Roblox is 17 to 24.[2]

Is Roblox merely this young generation's version of *The Oregon Trail*, an educational video game developed in the 1970s for boomer children to learn about the harsh realities of frontier life? Is it a spin-off of *SimCity*, a wildly popular video game among Gen X youth that simulated life in the city through building construction and other activities? Is it what *Minecraft* was for millennials? Or is it more than that? Virtual platforms like Roblox are an indicator that humanity continues to develop along a trajectory that blurs the line between physical and digital reality. To many people, and especially in unique ways for youth who are still forming their understanding of the world, what happens in the virtual world is as meaningful as what happens in the physical world because these circumstances reflect one another so closely. What is meaningful to people is what is real to them. And, for today's generation, environments and space are now forming the *metaverse*—an interactive interchange between the physical and virtual worlds.

This chapter does not argue that church life should necessarily be mirrored in virtual space—the metaverse is much more complex than that. Some churches, to be sure, have created virtual worship services where people can "attend" via their digital avatars.[3] But the heart of the debate around digital ministry is not methodological; it is anthropological, theological, and even missiological. Here are the contours of the issue: What is real human interaction, and can it happen digitally? Can people have genuine interaction with God digitally? If both human and divine digital interaction are indeed possible, then the church of today needs to become more aware that a monumental transition is happening in our midst. This shift is parallelling, and perhaps even overtaking, the shift of the global population from rural to urban.[4]

When considering digital ministry and church life, church leaders shouldn't simply ask, "*What* can we do and *how* can we do it?" but they should first ask *if* and *why* we should do something and *where* the metaverse is taking us. Indeed, there is a lot of open turf ahead. As Figure 8.1 shows, the majority of churches do online ministry, but this is largely limited to hosting the worship service online.

Figure 8.1—Few Churches Offer Digital Ministry Beyond Worship

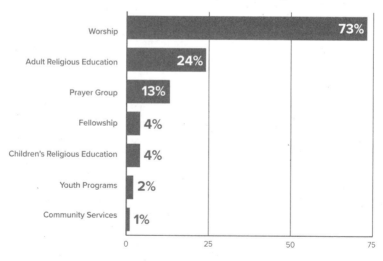

Offered *both* online and in-person during 2023

"Exploring the Pandemic Impact on Congregations" (EPIC), sponsored by Hartford Institute for Religion Research, adapted from Figure 9 (page 8) and Figure 14 (page 13), 2023; image courtesy ECFA.

Is Digital Ministry a Theological Advancement?

There might be no more important theological distinction Christians have from other religions and belief systems than the doctrine of the incarnation. It holds that, in Jesus of Nazareth, the one Creator God of the universe became human. The Gospel of John succinctly states the doctrine in this way:

> In the beginning was the Word, and the Word was with God, and the Word was God. . . . And the Word became flesh and dwelt among us, and we have seen his glory, glory as of the only Son from the Father, full of grace and truth. (John 1:1, 14)

The incarnation is so powerful because it explains why the universe that is full of potential exists: because the transcendent God intended to condescend himself and become σὰρξ or *sarx*—flesh, body, human nature—affirming the importance of humanity by matching our condition. John concludes from the sophisticated Greek worldview that the *Word* or *logos*—the nonphysical mind and divine reason of the cosmos—is personified.

Moreover, not only is God, in Jesus, matching the human physical condition, but he actually "dwelt among us," affirming our experiences and the things we call reality. Jesus felt compassion (Matt. 14:14), joy (Heb. 12:2), fear (Heb. 5:7), pressure (Luke 12:50), trouble (John 11:33; 12:27), and deep distress (Mark 14:33). He was also angry at times, such as when the Pharisees opposed his healing of a man with a deformed hand on the Sabbath (Mark 3:5). Hebrews 4:15 adds about Jesus, "For we do not have a high priest who is unable to sympathize with our weaknesses, but one who in every respect has been tempted as we are, yet without sin."

Reality isn't just physical matter, but also experiences created by humans in all of their forms. God "realized" himself alongside humanity, henceforth affirming reality as experienced by humans in all of our places and spaces.

But does this make ministry in nonphysical spaces and through nonphysical means mandatory? Let's first ask three clarifying questions:

- While virtual spaces do not physically exist, is it right to consider them "real" spaces to conduct meaningful human activity such as spiritual development and Christian community?
- The incarnation of God speaks to his embodied nature, but should we understand that he also occupies virtual spaces that humans inhabit, in the ways we inhabit them?
- Are virtual identities such as online avatars and social media profiles simply extensions of our physical identities, or are they becoming more intrinsic and integral components to who we are?

How we answer these questions, and others like them, form the ethical reasons—including the theological and philosophical perspectives—needed to answer the "what" and "how" questions of digital ministry. An increasing number of Christians are giving a resounding "yes" to questions like these without many caveats or qualifiers.

In their book *Networked Theology: Negotiating Faith in Digital Culture* authors Heidi Campbell and Stephen Garner challenge Christians to think of digital technology as a part of a larger ecological system rather than simply as tools or techniques. They say we should view technology as a dynamic and evolving system comprising diverse and interconnected entities and relationships. They propose:

An ecological view of technology may provide novel ways of connecting theological concepts described using pastoral and agrarian metaphors with contemporary technological issues. As such, a definition of technology as a system of God, people, practices, values, and technological artifacts in a particular local environment serves as a useful starting place for theological engagement.[5]

In the times and worldview of the Bible, its authors drew heavily from pastoral (i.e., animal care) and agrarian metaphors because these represented the ecological system they inhabited. God's creation of humanity as a farming couple that emerged from a garden made sense to the vast majority of the world. Likewise, teaching spiritual truths through parables about sowing and harvesting grain was an effective way for Jesus to talk about the life cycle of spiritual growth. Calling Jesus the Good Shepherd (John 10:11, 14) was a calming picture because readers understood what it meant to be led that way. Even now in the twenty-first century, the primary office of a church leader is still referred to as "pastor."

The rise of digital technology, then, is not the opposite of an agrarian worldview but an indicator and reminder that our metaphors for spirituality always accommodate our human experience because our tools, techniques, and technologies shape and transform this experience. Digital ministry will not only push church leaders in their techniques for ministry, but it will also push theologians in how they imagine and articulate the Christian worldview.

Just as Western missionaries once saw that advancing the cause of God's kingdom would mean boarding ships to explore (and unfortunately at times to exploit) new places

> Digital ministry will push theologians in how they imagine and articulate the Christian worldview.

and spaces, so the growing digital frontier presents itself as a place and space—maybe better understood as an aspect or dimension—of the kingdom of God that should be cultivated not *for* God but *with* God. If virtual spaces are real spaces after all, then the incarnation reminds us that God has already intended to occupy these spaces with us. This entails not just the discipleship aspect of digital ministry but also the missional and missiological aspect.

Bryce Ashlin-Mayo, dean of theology and associate professor of pastoral theology at Ambrose University in Calgary, Alberta, asks a practical yet provocative question in his book *Digital Mission: A Practical Guide for Ministry Online*: "Is there something flawed in your ecclesiology and missiology if your congregants live more and more of their lives online but their church refuses to enter this space?"[6] Perhaps the unwilling-ness of many to explore where digital ministry and mission will take the church is not rooted in a commitment to biblical fidelity and the possible aspects and dimensions of the kingdom of God. Rather, this reluctance is more of an unmovable or unintentional clinging to a particular way of doing church and ministry because previous generations were most used to this method. More importantly, many lack practical imagination or know-how even when they are willing to change.

As long as they do not mindlessly mirror technological trends of culture, today's thoughtful pioneers and practitioners of digital ministry will find themselves the forebears of the digital frontier over the next few decades. As church leaders attain more real-life experience through digital ministry and mission, those who record and recollect the spiritual fruit of these opportunities will be mapmakers and theologians, describ-ing both how and why God has come to be with us in a new, irrevocably digital age.

Participating in the Expanding Metaverse

How should church leaders advise church members on the usage of virtual spaces, particularly social media? The range of options is wide. Most would prefer their members to be constantly discerning, while some (perhaps a small minority) would prefer members to abstain from social media usage altogether. Regardless, the growing acceptance and embrace of social media as a part of church life is a gauge reminding us that we are merely at the beginning of understanding how digital media can and should be integrated in the Christian life, even while we do not yet fully understand its multigenerational impact.

Those who envision social media as primarily large public networks, such as Facebook, Instagram, Twitter, TikTok, or Snapchat, are likely unaware of the biggest emerging trend, which will impact how social media shapes identity and community for the future: smaller and more private social network groups. Mark Zuckerberg, founder and CEO of

Facebook, forecast the future direction of not just Facebook but social networks in general:

> Today we already see that private messaging, ephemeral [short-lived] stories, and small groups are by far the fastest growing areas of online communication. There are a number of reasons for this. Many people prefer the intimacy of communicating one-on-one or with just a few friends. People are more cautious of having a permanent record of what they've shared. And we all expect to be able to do things like payments privately and securely.
>
> Public social networks will continue to be very important in people's lives—for connecting with everyone you know, discovering new people, ideas and content, and giving people a voice more broadly. People find these valuable every day, and there are still a lot of useful services to build on top of them. But now, with all the ways people also want to interact privately, there's also an opportunity to build a simpler platform that's focused on privacy first.[7]

Larger apps are now becoming more associated with connecting users to brands and social media influencers. Smaller groups and apps afford users a sense of community and privacy.[8] After two decades of social media, users are collectively maturing and becoming more savvy in how they manage their digital media so that their virtual lives are more positively impacting their physical lives.

Mesfin Awoke Bekalu, research scientist in the Lee Kum Sheung Center for Health and Happiness at Harvard University's T. H. Chan School of Public Health, studied three aspects of social media usage: 1) social well-being, 2) positive mental health, and 3) self-rated health. His study—which reflected a nationally representative sample—showed that the routine usage of social media has positive effects on these three aspects when users are not so emotionally connected to their social media apps. High frequency usage of social media, therefore, does not have to lead to negative health. Instead, for mindful users, routine usage increases connection and compensates for diminishing face-to-face time due to busy lives.[9] This situation might be an indication that people are just now graduating from what might be framed as "phase one" of understanding and gaining mastery over social media. If true, this progress will eventually lead to a more meaningful and irreversible metaverse reality. This seems like a positive development from the days when FoMO first became a "thing."

Fear of missing out (FoMO) as a term was introduced in 2004 to describe the phenomenon observed on social networking sites. An academic article on the relationship between FoMO and mental health describes FoMO as including two processes: a perception of missing out followed up with a compulsive behavior to maintain these social connections.[10] The researchers of the report explore how FoMO develops out of a need to belong and form stable relationships. Although the article considers FoMO a type of problematic attachment to social media, associated with a range of negative life experiences and feelings ranging from poor sleep to difficulties in social functioning and neurobiological development, it also clarifies that FoMO is an indicator of how social media shapes perception of reality and personal identity.

> FoMO is an indicator of how social media is shaping perception of reality and personal identity.

FoMO is blurring the lines between who people are and how they perceive themselves in both physical and virtual reality. This concept also continues to remind us that digital media creates "real" places and spaces outside of the physical.

Over the two decades since FoMO was identified, more than 2,700 English-language academic dissertations and articles have covered this topic.[11] The continuous present-day research reminds us of two things: 1) our current gap in understanding the generational impact social media has on personal identity formation and socialization; and 2) the growing influence social media has on how we perceive reality. Society is still trying to understand what digital technology is doing to us, where it is taking us, and if the lines are being blurred between created and creator.

Predicting the convergence of human identity and technology feels adventurous and apocalyptic. Regardless of religion or spiritual background, many naturally feel trepidation in trying to discover the line that separates human identity and machines. However, many enthusiasts, Christians included, show great interest in a more transhuman future where technological development becomes integral to humans reaching their maximum potential.[12] Transhumanism is a movement from multiple disciplines that advocates the use of current and emerging technologies—such as genetic engineering, cryonics, artificial intelligence (AI), and nanotechnology—to augment human capabilities and improve the human condition.[13]

Arguments exist on both sides as to why church leaders should advance or abandon a more transhuman future, which inevitably spills into how favorable church leaders feel about digital advancement and the integration of digital media into everyday life. Regardless of where a church leader falls on this spectrum, effective church leadership for the future requires a more advanced understanding of how people today are developing their social identity and daily practice through digital media and technology. The metaverse is no longer just a piece of technology to master but is now also a social space to explore and cultivate.

Digital Currency and AI

A similar trajectory exists for the usage and integration of other digital media such as digital property and, especially, currency. Unlike traditional online banking through debit and automated clearing house (ACH) payments, which represent physical currency such as the United States dollar, cryptocurrency is digital-only currency. Unlike game currencies such as Robux, which works only in the Robloxian universe, cryptocurrency works in the physical world. Some church leaders are just now gaining curiosity as to how the digital economy will impact their church's mission.

Giving platforms such as Engiven are growing because they embrace the reality of cryptocurrency for churches and ministries. Engiven claims to be the number-one donation platform for stocks and cryptocurrency.[14] In an interview with Pushpay, another digital giving platform targeting churches, the cofounder and CEO of Engiven, James Lawrence, explains how churches and ministries will need to navigate the growing reality of cryptocurrency:

> We live in a culture that is now dominated by all things digital. While many aspects of generosity are still very relational, the process of giving and the transfer of assets is rapidly changing to an electronic methodology. . . .
>
> With the emergence of cryptocurrency, the giving process is not only 100% digital, but it also has what I would call "wonderful complexities." Engiven was founded to come alongside churches and nonprofits to educate and enable them to reduce these giving complexities so that they can harness a new asset class to the benefit of their mission.[15]

Just as it is becoming less common to see physical cash giving happen throughout church services, it is possible that cryptocurrency may become a common, if not a preferred way, to give large donations to churches and ministries in the future, especially from younger higher-income earners. If cryptocurrency achieves more stability over the next few years, churches that are not embracing this reality will need to climb a steeper learning curve as they figure out the future of generosity and capital campaigns. The future of financial portfolios among congregants and donors is highly likely to include cryptocurrency.[16]

The future of financial portfolios among congregants and donors is highly likely to include cryptocurrency.

However, what is likely even more misunderstood—or least engaged with—compared to social media and cryptocurrency is how artificial intelligence will impact the everyday life of Christians and the church. According to a 2023 study, *AI & The Church Survey*, sponsored by Gloo—a networking organization that connects faith-based organizations with reliable information, largely through technology—a majority of church leaders are *somewhat* to *very uncomfortable* with the emergence of AI in the world. A majority (54%) of those surveyed feel uncomfortable, 32 percent feel positive or excited, and 14 percent feel neutral. And while only 7 percent assert that AI should be condemned in church ministry, only 27 percent on the other side have a positive disposition toward the use of AI in the church.[17]

Gloo's findings can be interpreted as church leaders cautiously evaluating the integration of AI into church life. For those least initiated, AI can feel like a threat to human autonomy. At the spiritual level, AI feels like a replacement or an attempt to copy the human soul. Therefore, we do not think it is invalid to feel that AI is "playing God" to some extent, and this issue raises as many questions and objections as it does answers and opportunities.

However, some church leaders dabbling with AI tools such as ChatGPT or Gemini have found them useful for everything, ranging from sermon research and creating memorable sermon titles and email subject lines to discipleship curriculum writing and even advice for ministry design such as ensuring greater security for children's ministries. More than that, Christians every day are already reliant on AI in their daily lives from their use of Amazon Alexa and similar products to chatbot support provided by utility companies or online retailers. The question is not so much if church leaders will find ways to integrate AI into ministry and church life; it is already happening.[18] Rather, how much more will church leaders leverage AI in the right ways to create God-honoring teaching, discipleship, and spiritual formation?

Jason Thacker, director of the research institute at the Ethics and Religious Liberty Commission of the Southern Baptist Convention, offers a helpful perspective on the way church leaders can help lead the conversation to a more responsible AI future:

Deep down each of us knows that this world is broken and that we are not adequate to fix it on our own. For most people in our society, the longing for something greater than ourselves to solve our world's problems and injustices is tied to some level of intelligence outside of ourselves, like AGI [artificial general intelligence]. We are, indeed, looking for a savior.[19]

While much still needs to be imagined and pioneered for how AI will be integrated into the life of the church, congregational leaders should view our desire to develop machine intelligence to help humanity as a reminder of our spiritual longing. If AI is not immediately relevant to our day-to-day ministry, it is at least a day-to-day reminder of our reliance on an intelligence beyond ourselves that ultimately is God.[20]

The Metaverse as a Path to Mission and *Communitas*

Our cultural discourse pertaining to the metaverse has now far exceeded simply using digital media as a marketing tool in the church, primarily for mass communication. In the early days of the internet, church leaders saw digital media as a more effective alternative to mass mailers and billboard signs. Email lists were developed to tell as many people as possible about the ministries of a church. As online streaming became more prevalent, digital media's mass communication also grew into mass distribution of worship services and other kinds of teaching content. Prior to the internet, TV or radio were popular for religious broadcasts, but now online streaming has provided an even more accessible platform for people to view church services without being there in person.

According to 2023 Pew Research Center data, a quarter of U.S. adults regularly watch religious services online or on TV, and most of them—two-thirds—are either "extremely satisfied" or "very satisfied" with the experience.[21] This insight represents what is already becoming a well-worn, somewhat seamless pathway from mailers, brochures, billboards, TV, and radio to everything today that encompasses church online.

When the COVID-19 pandemic happened and nations went into

lockdown, what seemed like a niche ministry for technologically savvy churches suddenly became the primary mode of ministry and mission for a majority of churches. According to the COVID 19 Church Survey One Year Report released in 2021 by Exponential and the Wheaton College Billy Graham Center, only 4 percent of churches surveyed in America were not streaming online services.[22] During the early days of the pandemic, churches were still thinking about how to grow their online viewership. They started counting the number of unique visitors and viewers as a primary metric for how many people they were engaging. Eventually, some began thinking about creative outreach through online workshops or webinars, offering baking classes, dinner parties, and the Alpha course through Zoom. This place of liminality (transitional-ness) brought about by the pandemic may have actually helped create communities of missionaries or a dynamic that missiologist Alan Hirsch calls *communitas*, borrowing from the anthropologist Victor Turner:

> *Communitas* in [Victor Turner's] view *happens* in situations where individuals are driven to find one another through a common experience of ordeal, humbling, transition, and marginalization. It involves intense feelings of social togetherness and belonging brought about by having to rely on one another in order to survive. . . .
>
> The related ideas of liminality and *communitas* describe the dynamics of the Christian community inspired to overcome their instincts to "huddle and cuddle" and instead form themselves around a common mission that calls them to a dangerous journey to unknown places—a mission that calls the church to shake off its collective securities and plunge into the world of action, where its members will experience disorientation and marginalization but also where they will encounter God and one another in a new way.[23]

The COVID-19 pandemic was the first time that many saw the digital frontier as something that needed to be explored, and those who did so were experiencing *communitas*. In reality, this sense of a digital frontier had long been brewing outside the church before the pandemic, and some church leaders had already been thinking of the virtual space way beyond a simple view of digital media as marketing and mass communication. While some considered them as fringe expressions and proofs of concepts, churches such as VR MMO Church[24] and GodSquad Church[25] had already been intentionally engaging people in virtual places and spaces years before the pandemic, facilitating church and discipleship through digital media spaces such as Twitch, Discord, and even virtual reality headsets.

Whether or not they choose an intentional digital strategy, institutions that have become reliant on an analog past will eventually have to make a mental shift similar to the company formerly called Facebook, which now refers to itself as Meta, a "Social Metaverse Company." Meta's stated strategy is not necessarily to grow products such as Facebook or Instagram but rather to "build technologies that help people connect, find communities and grow businesses,"[26] in line with its mission of "giving people the power to build community and bring the world closer together."[27]

Additionally, while the bottom lines and motivations may not match, the purpose and the mission of the church in leveraging technology for the gospel could result in a similar vision to some leading technology companies—flourishing communities with integrity. Isn't this something the church should also be passionate about? The following story is an example of a church that wouldn't exist without the digital world.

Imagine Church

A DIGITAL CONGREGATION CREATES
ONSCREEN FACE-TO-FACE COMMUNITY

Janae and Justin Klatt, co-lead pastors of Imagine Church in Gilbert, Arizona, originally planned to lead a congregation in a typical brick-and-mortar setting. They started in 2017 by meeting on Sunday nights in a local church facility in the Phoenix suburb, but they also had family and friends from out of state who wanted to support them.

One of these friends eventually asked how the church would keep out-of-state supporters involved. In response, Janae Klatt, who is also the church's chief culture officer, drew on her earlier experience working at an international corporate job where Zoom video meetings were a regular way of communicating. "What if we just Zoom them into our launch team meetings, which would allow us to keep them up to date until some of them move here, and then we'll just continue in the brick and mortar?" she recalled suggesting.

However, something unexpected happened as the pastoral couple ordained in the Foursquare Church, a Pentecostal denomination, gathered for worship and online participants from California, New York, and Oklahoma joined in. "We started realizing that they were responding differently to the messages because of where they were located, and their context was different," Janae said. "And then, specifically, on one of the nights I was preaching I felt like the Holy Spirit said, 'Stop and ask a question, and then let everybody talk about it before you pick back up on your sermon.'"

This "weird" approach, as the Klatts initially considered it, turned into a key part of their digital strategy, an aspect that echoed the discussions they had sought to foster when they were youth pastors. "The result was groundbreaking," Janae commented regarding the predominantly white and multiethnic church that includes members who meet in half a dozen community groups totaling about 100 people.

The Klatts gained a wider understanding of their fellow worshipers by simply reading a portion of Scripture and asking participants to consider what the verses meant to them. For instance, according to Justin, the people watching via Zoom in Los Angeles related the Scripture to how they should care for their community in the midst of wildfires that were occurring in their state at the time. "It was like, whoa, they are contextualizing the sermon for themselves," he recalled. "We're not preaching from LA, and yet they are able to pastor each other and discuss with each other and disciple each other. This is *church*."

The Klatts never looked back, realizing the difference being made by pausing their sermons so discussions and thoughts could percolate before they continued their 30-minute on-screen messages. Now, they are what online church expert Chestly Lunday calls a "digital church using a digital-micro strategy as their primary gathering."

The church's digital "communities" are usually eight to twelve people meeting, as the Klatts like to call it, "face-to-face"—generally by seeing all the faces on a screen without needing to scroll up or down to see everyone. The Klatts do not want their communities to go much beyond a *Brady Bunch* level of involvement—this iconic '60s–'70s show used a similar grid of nine images in its opening title sequence for each episode. "After nine boxes on a screen, it's just too much," said Justin, "and then it's not real community." The Klatts hope that when a community group grows to about a dozen, another group will form so the small-group feel continues.

The online boxes of each group are filled with people who live in different parts of the country but who are committed to meeting at a particular time, whether it's midday Saturday or one of several weekday options. The age range is from young adults to people decades older—including Justin's former fourth-grade teacher. "The Saturday community is people from Virginia to Canada to Vegas to Arizona to California," he remarked concerning one of the ways people gather online across several time zones. Community members also stay connected throughout the week via a phone app, where they have their own chat channel and can share prayer requests and other information.

Each community has one or two "community builders" and "assistant community builders" who help facilitate their group. One community includes family members who live in different parts of the country and gather with others coping with health issues, such as a four-time cancer survivor and a man with multiple sclerosis who can't leave his home.

About once a quarter, the communities meet together for an "Imagine Live" service, where they pray, have a Communion service (where participants are encouraged ahead of time to gather with crackers and juice), and see more than the usual number of faces. At one such service, they prayed for missionaries from within their church who lived in Idaho and were headed to Bolivia.

Other rituals have included an online memorial service for the wife of a member. A flight attendant in that community had a layover where the member lived, and after other members gathered close to $500 for an Uber Eats gift card, she dropped it off in person at the man's house.

Baptisms also have a personal touch, even if it's from a nonmember. Justin, 44, recalled that a woman who wanted to be baptized suggested that her husband, who was not a Christian, assist her in their bathtub. "What if he was the one that dunked me while you guys are all on the call, praying over me and you are the ones to verbalize the baptism?" the woman asked the Klatts. "We're like, 'Yeah, let's do it,'" Janae recalled. "And he baptized his wife and the community rallied around and prayed for her."

The church also marks its birthday every year with an online party. "Every spring, we all open our birthday boxes together and pull out Imagine stickers and hats and shirts," Justin said.

Imagine Church has one brick-and-mortar site in Joseph City, Arizona, a rural location with a community center where about a dozen people meet. The only other local house of worship is a Mormon ward—a congregation affiliated with the Church of Jesus Christ of Latter-day Saints. The church formerly had other local venues, including in Tennessee and California, but the Klatts admit that the nature of their church concedes an ebb and flow in physical participation. "They have kind of a shelf life that's a lot shorter and smaller than the digital platform," said Janae, 41.

The Klatts, who both have Pentecostal ministers as parents, acknowledge that it's been a sacrifice to move from in-sanctuary to on-screen church. "We miss giving everybody a hug," Janae admitted. "It's weird preaching straight to a camera when there's no one in the room. That's a different dynamic."

Justin and Janae record their preaching in a studio that they created from a renovated garage space at their home. They often speak to an in-person audience of one: each other. A worship band, which lives in a bus and travels around the country, records the music for the service wherever it happens to be located. A video producer in Virginia edits the music and the message, inserting space for the discussions. During these conversations, there is a timer on the screen so those watching know when it is almost time to move on from discussion to continue hearing the rest of the sermon.

"I think the thing that has pushed us to keep going are the people who cannot get to traditional church," Janae said. "Being a PK, a pastor's kid, I didn't recognize the vast amount of people that cannot or will not walk through the doors of a church."

Rather than assuming that everyone wanted to be in church or had someone to invite them to church, Janae discovered a new mission field. "I started seeing people who are hungry for community, hungry for the church—for the big C church—and hungry for the people of God, but they don't know where to find them," she said. "They don't have the background in which to locate a healthy church or they don't have friends with those resources. And, so, that is the thing that drives me to preach past the camera and to the other side."

Creating Healthy Virtual Community

Perhaps more than any other organizational entity on earth, the local church could be society's research and development arm toward what could become the future's most meaningful metaverse spaces for belonging, identity formation, and emotional healing. If the church can get beyond thinking of digital spaces as just avatars on a screen or streaming services to "attend" online, it might see the metaverse as a new plane—or even a new planet of sorts—where people can digitally explore the grandeur of God and the potential of human goodness.

The metaverse is not a better version of physical reality, because that would mean it is only a virtual extension of it. But just as play therapy and other imaginative modalities have helped therapists unlock the potential in their patients and clients, the metaverse has the potential to unlock ways to imagine God that are unimaginable in an analog world. The omnipresent God is much more easily imagined in a metaphysical world. Recognizing how God is making the difference in any moment and in any place is intrinsic to the very existence of the church. This idea needs to be imagined from inside the metaverse. If only technologists, programmers, entrepreneurs, politicians, and ethicists imagine the human possibilities in the metaverse, this world could potentially be a reality that lacks any awareness of God's presence and activity. But if the church is meeting with Immanuel—God with us—in the early stages of the metaverse's development, then this imaginative world will be much more real because God's people are in it.

> **This imaginative world will be much more real because God's people are in it.**

The most committed readers of C. S. Lewis will know that he was unafraid to imagine outer space exploration and he remained open to life on other planets. Some of his thoughts are reflected in his Space Trilogy: *Out of the Silent Planet, Perelandra,* and *That Hideous Strength.* In an interview with journalist Sherwood Eliot Wirt about heaven, earth, and outer space, Lewis said:

> I look forward with horror to contact with the other inhabited planets, if there are such. We would only transport to them all of our sin and our acquisitiveness, and establish a new colonialism. I can't bear to

think of it. But if we on earth were to get right with God, of course, all would be changed. Once we find ourselves spiritually awakened, we can go to outer space and take the good things with us.[28]

Although the metaverse is not the same thing as life on other planets, Lewis is right in his observation that whatever exists beyond our everyday human reality would be tainted by our sin as we explore and we would only establish a new colonialism in these new worlds. But if we were to get right with God, we could take good things with us into these places and spaces. If there is real life in virtual reality, then the church will naturally be responsible to bring the gospel to the ends of the metaverse!

One Degree of Change⅘

Next are simple statements adapted from various ideas presented in this chapter about how church ministry will be different because of the expanding role of virtual platforms. Use the scale below each statement to assess how much you agree with it, choosing one answer for each row. Then begin some leadership conversations by comparing how much your responses align with the outlook of others in your church. There is space at the bottom of each list item for you to jot down any thoughts or ideas.

1. **Today's exploding world of digital media is likely to be as world-changing as the impact of the printing press or the shift from agrarian life to urban life.**

☐	☐	☐	☐	☐
STRONGLY DISAGREE	DISAGREE	UNCERTAIN OR NO OPINION	AGREE	STRONGLY AGREE

2. Digital ministry will significantly push us in how we imagine and articulate a Christian worldview.

☐	☐	☐	☐	☐
STRONGLY DISAGREE	DISAGREE	UNCERTAIN OR NO OPINION	AGREE	STRONGLY AGREE

3. Our church could do a better job of presenting the metaverse as a new planet of sorts where people can digitally explore the grandeur of God and the potential of greater human goodness.

☐	☐	☐	☐	☐
STRONGLY DISAGREE	DISAGREE	UNCERTAIN OR NO OPINION	AGREE	STRONGLY AGREE

4. Our church could do a better job of encouraging members to engage with people's spiritual longing that's being expressed in digital platforms.

☐	☐	☐	☐	☐
STRONGLY DISAGREE	DISAGREE	UNCERTAIN OR NO OPINION	AGREE	STRONGLY AGREE

5. Our church leadership does a good job in modeling a responsible use of digital media such as the avoidance of online quarreling, spreading disinformation, etc.

☐	☐	☐	☐	☐
STRONGLY DISAGREE	DISAGREE	UNCERTAIN OR NO OPINION	AGREE	STRONGLY AGREE

6. Our church leadership is actively equipping church members, especially parents with young children, on how to be wise about the consumption of social media and similar platforms.

☐	☐	☐	☐	☐
STRONGLY DISAGREE	DISAGREE	UNCERTAIN OR NO OPINION	AGREE	STRONGLY AGREE

7. Our church leadership has identified key groups of potential believers who are difficult to engage through in-person activities but might be open to virtual experiences we create.

☐	☐	☐	☐	☐
STRONGLY DISAGREE	DISAGREE	UNCERTAIN OR NO OPINION	AGREE	STRONGLY AGREE

BECOMING A FUTURE-READY CHURCH

CHAPTER 9

From Numbers to Vitality

WHY WE NEED NEW METRICS AND MODELS FOR CHURCH GROWTH

Dated question: How are we doing in terms of attendance, budget, and facilities?

Better question: How is God at work through various modes of church, and how can we become more aligned with healthy ways to grow the church?

THE TREND: Seeking church growth not by holding fast to one particular model but by embracing all the modes of the church.

Shift #8: In the past, many church leaders spent a lot of their time learning methods and techniques to grow their local congregation to reach its greatest potential size—typified by one big group in a church sanctuary. However, more and more leaders are now open to seeing how God is at work through different models of church outside of their own. Going forward, in order to reach a city or a region, church leaders will need to learn how to embrace the many modes of church and work collaboratively with others to transform a community.

Will Generations Z and Alpha measure church growth and health in exactly the same way as previous generations? With the rise of megachurches, there's no reason to think that the future of churches in America won't include large congregations. However, with the growing popularity and sustainability of microchurch movements, there's also no reason to think we've exhausted the possibility of new and smaller church expressions. We are at a time in American church history, perhaps more now than ever, when new churches and church leaders are, within the prescriptions of the Bible, pushing the boundaries of what the church can look like.

Grace and her husband, Sung, are a millennial church-planting couple who just celebrated another anniversary of their young church, which had launched during the COVID-19 pandemic. They recall how nervous they were trying to time the first service to match when their governor would loosen restrictions on in-person gatherings.

Even after their church started, Grace and Sung continued having monthly Zoom coaching calls with Ronnie, a church-planting mentor whose congregation had quickly become a megachurch in its first decade. As Grace and Sung recounted their ups and downs of their first years in church planting, they couldn't help but wonder how Ronnie's thirty-year-old church had grown so big and so fast.

At one point, Grace asked Ronnie, "How did you know when to multiply or shut down a small group or a campus?"

"If it wasn't healthy, then we shut it down," responded Ronnie. "If it was healthy, then God grew it, because healthy things grow."

Healthy things grow.

This was a popular twentieth-century mantra embraced in organizational leadership, especially within the Church Growth Movement (CGM) that emerged out of the 1970s. The CGM was a network of teaching churches, ministry consulting firms, conferences, and publications focused on helping pastors develop vision, leadership skills, and ministry strategies to increase the outreach and size of their congregations.[1] Over the years, a cottage industry developed around church health and growth, becoming one of the key markers and contributions of boomer and Gen X church leadership. In some circles, particularly among evangelicals, it would be difficult to imagine a twenty-first century local church without the influence of the CGM.

Just as there are vital signs indicating that a human body has life, including temperature, pulse rate, breathing rate, and blood pressure, likewise there are vital signs—or ecclesial minimums—for a church, including gatherings for worship and communion, biblical instruction, internal harmony, and public witness (Acts 2:42–47). While these vital indicators for the church are not up for debate in the history of Christianity, the CGM sought to generate and evaluate the quality, intensity, and efficiency in which local churches experienced them. It offered tools and standards to manage and measure outcomes of the church.

Some have criticized the CGM for its pragmatism or the way it interpreted certain principles, while others have either held fast or adapted its ideas into other streams of missional ministry and church leadership development.[2] While study of healthy church growth certainly has not disappeared, it has been codified into much of the modern church. Thus, it is time in North American missiology to propose fresh methodologies appropriate for our cultural moment—perhaps even for the next. To do this requires a reality check for how the church actually exists in our social imagination and how we have chosen to manage it as an entity.

> It is time to propose fresh methodologies appropriate for our cultural moment.

New Testament Church versus Nonprofit Corporation

The language of organizational health and growth is particularly relevant to the modern church partly because the dominant paradigm for most local churches is the nonprofit organization (or, to use the legal term, religious corporation). While most pastors and church leaders would prefer to think of themselves as spiritual leaders of organic communities, by definition, many of them are de facto corporation leaders of legal entities accountable to both state and federal governments (which allows for tax-deductible donations). This is an observation more than a value judgment on churches primarily functioning as a nonprofit corporation. (In general, we affirm that churches in the modern, Western, and democratic world are better off when they are accountable to a supportive, yet secular government that values religious diversity and freedom. They may also benefit from accountability to networks such as the Evangelical Council for Financial Accountability.)

From a governmental perspective, nonprofit entities provide a social service for the common good and therefore are given tax-exempt status in exchange. This means that churches are adjacent to businesses and other institutions in the eyes of the government and our socioeconomic system. They are largely undifferentiated from organizations such as a United Way chapter or an Islamic community center. The way an entity

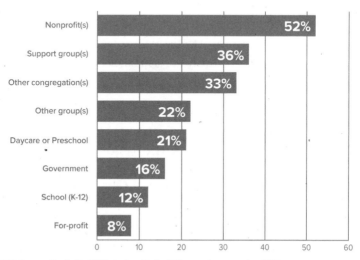

Figure 9.1—Many Churches Share Their Facilities

Congregations that rent or donate space
to one or more of the following

Nonprofit(s) **52%**
Support group(s) **36%**
Other congregation(s) **33%**
Other group(s) **22%**
Daycare or Preschool **21%**
Government **16%**
School (K-12) **12%**
For-profit **8%**

Faith Communities Today, 2020, analyzed by Scott Thumma; image courtesy ECFA.

is understood and held accountable by authorities partly determines how the entity leaders view and understand themselves.[3] And, indeed, churches are increasingly sharing their facilities with community organizations, as Figure 9.1 illustrates. Some get their space for free, some for a fee, and some for exchanged services.

At the same time, church leaders must also remind themselves that while their churches are similar to other organizations in structure and incorporation, the church is different in *essence*. This means that the church should not be measured and evaluated in the same exact ways.

However, the model of church that looks like a growing and complex nonprofit organization requires layers of skill and competency for present and future church leaders. As the decades go by, it is becoming increasingly difficult for leaders to have all the skill sets necessary to shepherd a growing organization while maintaining the spiritual resilience and moral integrity required for biblical office. Unfortunately, churches have often outgrown the character of their leaders.[4]

Furthermore, complexity has led to a greater professionalization of church ministry, as the new kinds of roles (whether volunteer or paid) emerging over the last few decades show: executive pastors, campus pastors, community engagement directors, missions pastors, church planting pastors, young adult ministers, youth/family/children pastors, digital pastors, communications directors, and more. (Not to mention the number of administrative and human resource staff positions that must be created.) These are not just people to shepherd but also positions to manage. Given the current trajectory, it is far more complex to lead a church in the twenty-first century than it was in the twentieth century.

Whether the church has five, five hundred, or fifty thousand people—and all those options exist today—church leaders will have to ask themselves whether the paradigm of an ever-growing and increasingly complex organization is inheritable by emerging leaders, especially given the current leadership models we

> It is far more complex to lead a church in the twenty-first century than it was in the twentieth century.

have. Or, as we mentioned in chapter 1, will it feel cumbersome to them like Saul's armor, which young David attempted to wear without success, saying, "I cannot go with these, for I have not tested them" (1 Sam. 17:39)?

Amid our very good intentions of recruiting more young people eager and capable to lead our prevailing paradigm of the church into the future, can we also afford to ignore those who decidedly "have not tested" it at all? Or will we now have enough vision and humility to honor and help young leaders receive their own imagination from God for how the kingdom can manifest through new expressions and models? Finally, can we do this by neither disregarding church growth models nor doubling down on them?

Motifs: First-Century Patterns for Twenty-First Century Practice

A good next step is to review some of the Bible's instructive and imaginative motifs for what the church can be like, especially as we move further into the twenty-first century. Naturally, each generation of the church is limited to a time and place in history, so church leaders draw out from Scripture what they need for meaning and direction for their time. For example, the idea of digital ecclesiology—much of what we discussed in the last chapter—would have made little sense prior to a few decades ago. However, today, especially after the COVID-19 pandemic, it is a burgeoning discourse that will only continue to grow.[5] We think about particular things in certain ways only because of the times in which we live.

Generations Z and Alpha will greatly benefit from paying particular attention to two aspects of a biblical imagination for the churches they will lead: faithful and fruitful. The Bible determines what the future church needs so it can be considered faithful and fruitful, and our present interpretation should not restrict new generations from dreaming up how "faithful and fruitful" can look different for them. Certainly future leaders must be concerned about the church's biblicality. *Is it worshipping? Are its members faithful to one another? Is it evangelistic?* But we should be honest and aware enough to disclose to them that our cultural captivity to models may need innovation and even liberation.[6] *Is this right for today but not for tomorrow? Is this right for us but not for them? Is God doing something new that hasn't been done before?* Permission to be free and to create is a part of future leaders' hermeneutics for discovering fresh meaning for prominent themes of the church in the New Testament—namely, family, body, temple, and fractal.

Future Church Feels Like Family

If people are experiencing church as family, they might say the following phrases to themselves:

We are not alone.
We belong to a people.
People belong to us.

We spent part of chapter 3 showing that the New Testament writers understood "family" to mean more than the nuclear family—it also included extended relatives, workers, and even the estate. And, in a way, the early church widened this idea of a family, going above and beyond biological relationships and ethnic heritage. The Old Testament included familial language to describe how the nation of Israel related to God. The new covenant in Christ went deeper to illustrate emotional and intimate experiences within the church, including interpersonal relationships, and gave a range of what we might feel when we belong one to another:

- "And stretching out his hand toward his disciples, [Jesus] said, 'Here are my mother and my brothers!'" (Matt. 12:49).
- "Love one another with brotherly affection. Outdo one another in showing honor" (Rom. 12:10).
- "Do not rebuke an older man but encourage him as you would a father, younger men as brothers, older women as mothers, younger women as sisters, in all purity" (1 Tim. 5:1–2).

- "To Timothy, my beloved child: Grace, mercy, and peace from God the Father and Christ Jesus our Lord" (2 Tim. 1:2).
- "For it is time for judgment to begin at the household of God; and if it begins with us, what will be the outcome for those who do not obey the gospel of God?" (1 Peter 4:17).

"Church as family" is not composed of convenient membership but of emotionally invested relationships. "Church as family" can also be thought of as the best sense of "church as really special friends." Just as the New Testament's churches endeavored, so churches led by the next generation will facilitate nearness, proximity, and kinship that quenches the loneliness bred by our culture of broken nuclear families. Churches should not grow beyond their practical ability to be intimate, and therefore ultimately a church often should not be just a crowd (even though it might *look* like a crowd from the outside). Rather, a church should be relationally rich, with bonds forged in passion and mission and proven over time as its members persevere through life's ups and downs.

Church as family strives to overcome codependency through interdependency. It is certainly filled with some people far into their journey of healing, but mostly with people wanting attachment—who often receive it imperfectly with disappointment but are always trying and always forgiving. Church as family—and as really special friends—is hard, but it is also healing.[7]

Future Church Operates Like a Body

We are contributors.
We complement each other.
Our size does not determine our significance.

The church is a paradox of sorts. Like the human body, its usefulness is in the strength of the sum of its parts, but its honor is often in the weakness of some of its parts (1 Cor. 12:22). It has personality and character and can occasionally get tired and weak. Its size is arbitrary and says very little about its faithfulness. To be big can mean either strong or bloated. To be small can mean either agile or sickly. As the next generation becomes less superficial about big versus small, it may finally stop body shaming the body of Christ. When Paul described God's church as a body, his primary reference point was not our modern church growth methodologies or our church size controversies. Instead, he was anchoring the church to the Word that took on flesh (John 1:14), which was alive and at work in the world:

> Rather, speaking the truth in love, we are to grow up in every way into him who is the head, into Christ, from whom the whole body, joined and held together by every joint with which it is equipped, when each part is working properly, makes the body grow so that it builds itself up in love. (Eph. 4:15–16)

The church is one of the few institutions in the West that is collectivistic, but it does not devalue the individual. By design it is not supposed to expend and exhaust people, just as a body should not expend and exhaust a body part. The present circumstances are teaching future leaders to understand well that a church crumbles under dictatorship but can never rise under spectatorship. At least in the workplace, Gen Z is not the snowflake generation stereotyped by popular media.[8] Yet, perhaps more so than previous generations, it expects greater levels of empathy from its leaders[9]— maybe because it has a healthier sense of shame. Self-care was a skill previous generations had to learn, but it is becoming instinctual for Gen Z. This is good news for the church as the body of Christ.

> A church crumbles under dictatorship but can never rise under spectatorship.

Future Church Is Structured as a Temple

We are a spiritual structure.
We host the Spirit of God.
We facilitate power.

Certainly the church is not fundamentally a building—yet Paul says it is a temple:

> You are fellow citizens with the saints and members of the household of God, built on the foundation of the apostles and prophets, Christ Jesus himself being the cornerstone, in whom the whole structure, being joined together, grows into a holy temple in the Lord. In him you also are being built together into a dwelling place for God by the Spirit. (Eph. 2:19–22)

Understanding the church as a reverent structure built upon Christ Jesus increases our awareness for humility and accountability. The authority contained in a structure is far more powerful than in any individual or a group of individuals. The apostolic impetus of emerging leaders will feel less like boomer and Gen X entrepreneurs. Leadership structures will feel flatter, and future leaders will pioneer ministry through presence like many of the trailblazing Jesuit and Moravian missionaries, allowing the form of their ministry to be shaped by the needs of those whom they are serving.

Future leaders' prophetic impetus may also be different from their millennial mentors. They will not feel the need to change the entire world—that seems too ambitious. Rather, they realize that their physical presence in a place represents something priestly. Future churches might also feel less critical of the world. Like early Amish and Mennonite communities, they prefer to offer themselves up to others as a quiet alternative to the chaotic culture.

Although it was brief, we were reminded by the Asbury University Outpouring that God is alive and active among a young priestly class desiring first and foremost to minister to him.[10] Their temple gatherings will be a brokerage or clearinghouse for power—Holy Spirit power. God will inhabit the praises of his people (Psalm 22:3) and they will be filled with the Spirit. And perhaps the greatest vital signs of the future church are how, through prayer and fasting (see Mark 9:29), evil power is destroyed among oppressors and uplifting power is generated among the gentle and lowly. Churches of the future reject accumulating power for themselves, instead disbursing it to the weak and vulnerable (Luke 4:16–19) as priests of the living temple of God.

Future Church Exists as a Fractal

> We are part of the Holy Trinity.
> "I in them and you in me."
> We are, together, reflecting Jesus's presence, even if just two or three.

Although there is no equivalent of the word *fractal* mentioned in the Bible, the pattern of God working in the world through relationships is both part of the story and also the entirety of the story. In mathematics, fractals are shapes—most often triangles—composing patterns, which still maintain the exact shape of the most basic frame, or fractal, when you scale up or down. For instance, imagine a triangle composed of triangles, which are also composed of triangles. This is a beautiful picture of the church that is the same in essence no matter what the space, place, size, or tradition may be.

The church's most basic frame is the relationship between the Father, the Son, and the Holy Spirit. Jesus prays this in John 17:22–23:

> The glory that you have given me I have given to them, that they may be one even as we are one, I in them and you in me, that they may become perfectly one, so that the world may know that you sent me and loved them even as you loved me.

Every instance, model, and expression of church reflects this fractal. This also reminds us that the church has been much more agile and fluid than we think. Despite our attempts over two thousand years to frame the church as a gathering in a house or an enmeshment with an empire, it has been both. Embracing this reality for the

> The church has been much more agile and fluid than we think.

future can help release the tension that many leaders in the recent past have felt when their church has not grown at the same rate as another down the street. Understanding church as fractal affirms the practicality of the universal church[11] while simultaneously honoring the smallest and simplest expressions of the church. After all, both aspects are patterned after the Holy "Triangle"—Father, Son, and Spirit.

Jesus also affirms in Matthew 18:20, "where two or three are gathered in my name, there am I among them." This statement alone does not mean that the totality of the church can be represented in a small setting of a few. However, the essence of what the church can be in the world does not need much more than a few inviting Jesus to be central to their life together. At its most basic essence, that was the project of God sending his Son into the world. Thus, Jesus illustrates the point that, just as the members of the Holy Trinity are few in number, it only takes a few cooperating friends to invoke the divine purpose and presence of God into a moment. If someone does not experience this reality at the level of two or three people, then he or she won't experience it at the level of two or three thousand people. Consequently, today in America we are seeing more churches like Church Project in Houston reimagine what it means to be a large church through valuing their house churches even more.

Church Project

MEGACHURCH DEVELOPS THROUGH A SERIES OF HOUSE CHURCHES

When he was growing up, Jason Shepperd attended what he considered a traditional church—with a very formal and "super-centralized" structure. However, the church he presently leads is truly modeled on the traditional church, created by Jesus when he preached to thousands—before the term "megachurch" became common parlance—and continued by his disciples who met in house churches.

"I think there are three predominant DNA elements that should be in every church across all peoples, all places, and all time," said Shepperd, founder and lead pastor of Church Project in The Woodlands, Texas. "They were in the early church, and they should be in all of our churches now—and they are not."

Since 2010 Shepperd, 50, has made his theory a reality, coining phrases for the key features of the series of house churches he's developed in a northern suburb of Houston. He says they are "decentralized from primary place" and feature "distributed pastoral leadership" and "diverse discipleship communities."

Starting with forty people over a decade ago, Shepperd now has between two and three thousand people involved in house churches. "We take a teacher, a Sunday school teacher, or a small group leader, and we elevate them and make them a pastor," he said. "And we take a class or a group and we elevate it and we make it a church."

What is the basis for "distributed pastoral leadership"? Shepperd points to the first chapter of Titus as a biblical example: "Paul told Titus to appoint elders in every town. He wanted a pastor available for all the people where they live. He did not want Titus to be the pastor for everyone and go to them, and he didn't want all the people to go to Titus."

The house churches of Shepperd's Church Project are guided by unpaid lay leaders. "You have firemen, doctors, engineers, and teachers, who are pastoring people," explained Shepperd. "They're doing weddings and funerals and benevolence, and all those things happen through house churches, not through a central primary place and priest. . . . It's a community of people who are meeting each other's needs."

According to Shepperd, the hosts of the house churches, in most cases, are not the house pastor and their families but others who have "radical gifts of hospitality."

And none of those involved are called "members." "Our goal is not membership," Shepperd asserted. "Our goal is full engagement in the life of the church."

Those who gather in a house church meet most Sunday or Wednesday evenings, preferably "the closest one and the night that works best for you." They are part of a total of 7,500 who are involved monthly in Shepperd's Church Project. They may also attend a weekly Sunday gathering where they hear him preach or take part in a service project working with area ministries that help people who are homeless or incarcerated.

The smaller intergenerational gatherings—with as many as thirty-five or forty people—in houses, and sometimes apartments, include a meal, discussion of the scriptural passage preached on at the large Sunday meeting, and prayer. "This is the time where people can wrestle with this and say, 'I'm not sure if I believe this,' 'I'm not applying this to my life,' or 'I'm not living the way that the Scripture is calling me to,'" Shepperd described. "We like to think that we have fifty, sixty, seventy prayer gatherings happening throughout the week all across our city."

Acknowledging that these gatherings can be "a little messy" as kids run in and out and a couple of adults take turns and use project-provided resources to work with the children, Shepperd wouldn't have it any other way. "We really love the idea that kids are seeing their parents with other believers studying the Bible and praying," he said. "But other than children, everybody is engaged in a house church together—old, young, rich, poor. Black, brown, Asian, white, married, and unmarried. Believer, immature believer, unbeliever—we're all together in this house church community."

The house churches are broader communities and not solely a weekly meeting of food, Bible study, and prayer. "They're going on vacations together, watching each other's kids together, and visiting people in the hospital together," Shepperd remarked.

But these house churches don't always succeed. "Sometimes people get tired. Sometimes they feel ill-equipped," Shepperd admitted.

"We have learned that we have to take care of our house church leadership better. And we've continued to adjust."

Neither a large weekly gathering nor a smaller house church atmosphere appeal to everyone who is part of Church Project. Some who are new to Christianity, or are getting reacquainted with it, are already making a big move by stepping into a room with two thousand other adults, according to Shepperd. "To take the next step—of getting into a living room with somebody—it might take a while for them to build some trust, and so there's generally a decent lag time," he added. "Conversely, there are some people who won't come to a building, but they will go to a house church."

In this "mega-micro hybrid," some people are baptized by their house church pastor at the large gatherings; others might prefer for the officiant to baptize them in a backyard pool. This sense of decentralization extends to the building where Shepperd preaches. "We're a church of thousands of people. We have no phone number. We have no receptionist in a foyer. Our building is not central to who we are," he explained.

Shepperd oversees seven full-time pastors who are guiding the house pastors. "Our staff is here to support and encourage, to walk alongside the house church pastor, and there are times where things happen where the house church pastor is not equipped for that—and we help them," Shepperd said. For instance, as part of Church Project's "distributed pastoral leadership," house church pastors are trained to officiate at funerals. However, under certain circumstances, such as "a tragedy with a young mother," the staff step in.

With staff offices occupying just 8 percent of the building, the structure may be used for free by local ministries and rented by businesses and schools during the week (a recent trend in some churches; see Figure 9.1). Church Project has redistributed to Christian ministries millions of dollars in donations it has received as a corporate entity.

With decentralized leadership and fewer staff (Shepperd estimates that the staff of Church Project is a quarter the size of a comparable traditional church) come more growth. "It's hard for us to tell people to stop coming to a house," he said. "So, our idea is when a house church gets too big, that hopefully we would have by then the house church pastor prepared and a host family prepared to multiply and send people out to start another house church."

Shepperd considers himself the pastor of "all the people" through his preaching and oversight, but he believes "the most important responsibility of a pastor is whom we entrust to pastor other people." That approach, he said, also leaves him less exhausted since he serves as a pastor more than as an organizational leader, which he said was the type of church role he held before starting Church Project. "I believe, actually, I will be able to endure as a pastor with excitement for all of my days ahead," he said. "I didn't feel this way in other models or approaches."

Models and Metrics: Reimagining What Could Be for Generation Z

Given the imagery of the church as a fractal (and as demonstrated by Church Project), we now need to look at how church leadership will likely develop over the next few decades, especially the period in which Gen Z will settle into senior- and executive-level leadership while boomers and Gen Xers lead from the side as coaches and champions.

All signs indicate that these five models of church will increasingly converge: mega, missional, multiethnic, micro, and meta, as Figure 9.2 illustrates. This does not mean that traditional churches are going away. In fact, the future church depends on current church models remaining but working together, borrowing and blending from each other. Already, the gap between these models and the thought leaders who have championed them over the last few decades seems to be closing. The current collaboration among them leads us to think that their convergence is imminent.

Figure 9.2—Blurring of Models Ahead

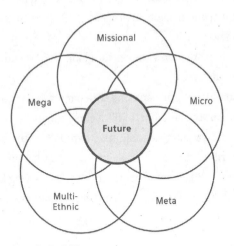

Model and image developed by Daniel Yang.

However, the greater point here is that Gen Z, like the generations before it, is simply stepping into its Spirit-led calling and responsibility to take the kingdom of God to *everywhere at every time*. The convergence of these models may be a part of how the kingdom is manifesting in America in the first half of the twenty-first century. Also, Gen Z may be better equipped with the intellectual and financial capital to lead this movement than any other generation before it. They will be in an even higher position when boomers, Gen Xers, and millennials maintain and increase social capital by being a good witness of the gospel to the world.

So, as many already suspect, the future will not get rid of the need to evaluate lag measures such as budgets, buildings, and baptisms. But it will challenge us to try to capture more long-term lead indicators of the kingdom of God at work. Many industries, especially organizations with a humanitarian focus, now have social performance indicators or metrics that help them measure the impact of their work in society independent of their bottom-line growth. These kinds of indicators and metrics keep organizations focused not only on the services they provide in the moment but also on how they impact a community for the long term. Therefore, organizations often are encouraged to be a part of an ecosystem of other entities and co-creative agents attempting to solve a similar issue or one relevant to it.[12]

One way to express how to measure long-term social impact is to ask, "Is this beautiful?"

Budgets, buildings, and baptisms are a part of making a community *beautiful*. Beauty is the new fourth "B" of church metrics. For some time, leaders have tried to get at a qualitative dynamic of the beauty of the church by describing it as influential, impactful, or having a good reputation. This dynamic is pointed out in Acts 2:47 as "having favor with all the people" and in the fifty-nine *one another* commandments in the New Testament,[13] which include:

- loving one another (Rom. 12:10; 1 Thess. 3:12; 1 Peter 1:22; 1 John 3:11)
- not passing judgment on one another (Rom. 14:13)
- living in harmony with one another (Rom. 15:5)
- instructing and admonishing one another (Rom. 15:14; Col. 3:16)
- caring for one another (1 Cor. 12:25)
- comforting and agreeing with one another (2 Cor. 13:11)
- serving one another (Gal. 5:13)
- bearing with one another (Eph. 4:2; Col. 3:13)
- being kind to one another, tenderhearted, forgiving one another (Eph. 4:32)
- addressing one another in psalms and hymns and spiritual songs (Eph. 5:19)
- submitting to one another (Eph. 5:21)
- not lying to one another (Col. 3:9)
- exhorting one another (Heb. 3:13)
- stirring up one another to love and good works (Heb. 10:24)
- encouraging one another (Heb. 10:25)
- not speaking evil against one another (James 4:11)

- not grumbling against one another (James 5:9)
- confessing sins to one another and praying for one another (James 5:16)
- showing hospitality to one another (1 Peter 4:9)
- clothed with humility toward one another (1 Peter 5:5)
- having fellowship with one another (1 John 1:7)

These are not subjective descriptions but are objective prescriptions to be experienced and measured. When practiced in totality, even if done imperfectly, this creates a *beautiful* church! This was the church that had favor among all people in Acts 2. It goes beyond influence, impact, and a good reputation; it is a qualitative measure of an existential reality. When a church strives to be beautiful, it will exist for the right length of time and for the right people. In their most primal essence, as outlined by the *one anothers*, churches are a reminder to the world what God has created humanity to be.

Revisiting the previous section regarding motifs, another way to understand the beauty of your church and how it is experienced in your community is to better understand . . .

- What is the *family* "rule of life" and routine that we promote? And does it increase belonging or potential estrangement?
- What kinds of unhealthy shame in the *body* do we need to deal with before it becomes toxic?
- Does the structure of our *temple* make room for the Spirit of God and empower the weak in our community?
- Are we fluid enough that our people can form *fractal* expressions of the church in the places they live, work, and play?

Metaskills: Three Roles Needed to Pivot

As church leaders of today continue to cultivate leaders for the brave new world of the future (which our book argues has already arrived), we hope to give readers a pinpoint issue to focus on, especially in regard to what is necessary for church leadership in the next decade or so.

Metaskills are abilities that are learned and applied relatively quickly. These aren't juxtaposed with what is called deep knowledge—understanding and wisdom about a subject that develops over time and experience. However, metaskills are what is necessary in a given moment to make a pivot or to make the one degree of necessary change for a more focused direction. They are the right tools for the right moment to build the ship and point it in that right direction of becoming future-ready.

Metaskill 1: Facilitating

Our current cultural moment requires strong leadership with the right tone and posture. Facilitators are able to be not only first-chair leaders but also second-chair leaders because they realize that the cultural moment requires less ego and fewer top-down decision makers. The skepticism toward institutions and establishments is currently shared across all generations. This does not mean that facilitators should always abdicate or defer, but they should be able to read the room to know when they should defer so others can rise up and take the lead. They are also much more inclined toward collaboration and co-creation because they know that they don't have all the information and resources needed to create long-term impact. Facilitators possess enough self-awareness to know their level of specialty and perhaps have a hunch about what others are good at. They have also developed an instinct of knowing how to create partnerships that center the whole rather than themselves.

> The cultural moment requires less ego and fewer top-down decision makers.

Metaskill 2: Healing

Trauma-informed methodologies have emerged in the church over the years not so much because of the rise in popularity of therapeutic modalities but because the pressure points are being released by so many unique cultural moments. Our understanding of healing in the church has become more holistic, encompassing the mental, physical, and social aspects of our spiritual nature. After all, healers know that there are always internal and external dimensions to an issue. They also understand the personal and systematic issues that bring harm to a community. Consequently, their path toward healing is both a posture of empathetic listening and gospel-informed living, which centers Christ at a person's healing. A leader who is a healer helps people overcome their frazzled deconstructive tendencies so they can focus on one point of healing and walk confidently on a path of reconstructing their faith and hope in the church.

Metaskill 3: Seeing

At the 2023 global gathering of the Movement Leaders Collective held in Chicago, over one hundred leaders of missional movements from around the world met together as a learning community. Brian Sanders, the cofounder of the Tampa Underground church—a network of microchurches—challenged the group by saying, "In a world filled with cynics, it is the optimist that is the prophet." Seers for this cultural moment are realists, but they are also romantics; love is always in the air for them. They may not have vision in the same way as entrepreneurial leaders, but they see both the world and people in a way that calls everyone up to a greater ideal. They don't lead by religious platitudes, but because they have met with God their encounters have created a humble confidence that the God of salvation is committed to redeeming the bride of Christ for the Bridegroom. Pessimists cannot see the future; only the seers can.

One Degree of Change 4

Next are simple statements adapted from various ideas presented in this chapter about church vitality and its different modes. Use the scale below each statement to assess how much you agree with it, choosing one answer for each row. Then begin some leadership conversations by comparing how much your responses align with the outlook of others in your church. There is space at the bottom of each list item for you to jot down any thoughts or ideas.

1. **Healthy churches grow over time, both in outreach and in size.**

☐	☐	☐	☐	☐
STRONGLY DISAGREE	DISAGREE	UNCERTAIN OR NO OPINION	AGREE	STRONGLY AGREE

2. **It is far more complex to lead a church in the twenty-first century than it was in the twentieth century.**

☐	☐	☐	☐	☐
STRONGLY DISAGREE	DISAGREE	UNCERTAIN OR NO OPINION	AGREE	STRONGLY AGREE

3. **The most important responsibility of a pastor today is whom to equip and entrust to pastor other people.**

☐	☐	☐	☐	☐
STRONGLY DISAGREE	DISAGREE	UNCERTAIN OR NO OPINION	AGREE	STRONGLY AGREE

4. Churches led by the next generation will facilitate nearness, proximity, and kinship that quenches the loneliness bred by our culture of broken nuclear families.

☐ STRONGLY DISAGREE ☐ DISAGREE ☐ UNCERTAIN OR NO OPINION ☐ AGREE ☐ STRONGLY AGREE

5. Emerging leaders will pioneer ministry through presence, allowing the form of their ministry to be shaped by the needs of those whom they are serving.

☐ STRONGLY DISAGREE ☐ DISAGREE ☐ UNCERTAIN OR NO OPINION ☐ AGREE ☐ STRONGLY AGREE

6. Future churches will operate more like how the body of Christ is intended to function.

☐ STRONGLY DISAGREE ☐ DISAGREE ☐ UNCERTAIN OR NO OPINION ☐ AGREE ☐ STRONGLY AGREE

Conclusion

IS THE NEXT GENERATION READING THIS BOOK WITH YOU?

The book *Into the Future* begins with the true story[1] of a little-traveled street just outside of town that's ideal for drag racing. It's a long, level, perfectly straight stretch that runs unchanged for more than two miles. The only challenge is to finish the race before the street takes a sharp turn . . . because otherwise the driver will land in a swamp that borders the curve.

One evening, local police received a report about a car stranded in the foot-deep waters of the swamp. Typically, the responding officer will find a slightly intoxicated teenager who didn't slow down enough to make the turn. This time it was a rather embarrassed elderly couple.

"How did this happen?" the officer asked the couple, after safely escorting them to the police car. The husband, who had been at the wheel, began explaining his difficulties in using his new trifocals. He simply couldn't get used to making the necessary mental adjustments.

In the end, he concluded, "I couldn't see, so I kept going the way I had been going!"

What a parallel for churches! Instead of negotiating the next bend in the road, our default is often not to try to improve our vision but to just keep going the same direction and speed, especially if the previous stretch of our church's journey was a relatively smooth stretch. Yet, somehow, too many churches land in the "swamp" before they gain enough focus on the future to realize that the road has turned another way and they have missed the navigation clues. *Becoming a Future-Ready Church* has been about having the conversations that will help you spot these clues and then take appropriate action.

Partnering with the Next Generation

Context matters. This book is full of backstories, each chapter attempting to get at the "why" behind the way we do ministry and what seems to be changing as we go forward.

Granted, God doesn't change. Nor does the gospel. But the issues that matter to each rising generation are in constant realignment. So are the topics that grab their attention. So are the ways they process information. Thus, the context is constantly changing.

The way people see the world today is not the same as they did in 1950. And by 2050 they will likely view it differently than they do today. For example, who could have predicted in 1950 that by 2023 the level of loneliness and isolation would be such a widespread mental health issue that the U.S. surgeon general would declare it to be at an "epidemic" level?[2] Increased loneliness is indicative of the mass cultural shifts happening in a relatively short period of time that are leaving people disoriented.

Wise church leaders will follow the model of those who led God's people in the past, "who had understanding of the times, to know what Israel ought to do" (1 Chr. 12:32).

Becoming a Future-Ready Church began with a brief tour of the 1950s, when most ministry models in use today originated. Then it guided you through eight different conversations that you need to start now in order to communicate the unchanging gospel to a society whose interests, thought patterns, and social needs are ever-changing. At the same time, this book has emphasized that a tremendous opportunity exists. As one

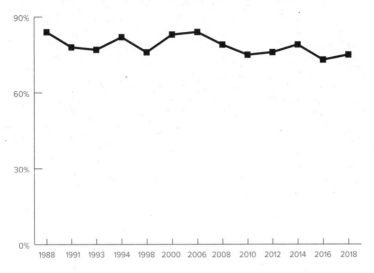

**Figure 10.1—Vast Majority of "Never Attenders"
Continue to Believe in God or a Higher Power**

General Social Survey, 1988–2018, analyzed by Ryan Burge; image courtesy ECFA.

way to affirm how reachable our neighbors are for spiritual discussions, Figure 10.1 shows that roughly four in five people believe in God or a higher power. Plus, that high percentage has not declined over time.

If this book has done its job, hopefully you're convinced that your church must involve its next generation of leaders in ongoing conversations that will help prepare you for the future. These discussions are intended to help you dig deeply into paradigm-shaping questions that will guide you in making a series of long-term adjustments to ministry strategy and actions, consequently causing purposeful change.

> **Your church must involve its next generation of leaders in conversations that will help prepare you for the future.**

Specifically, we suggested a new set of questions to talk about as your church makes necessary shifts. We identified specific questions for each of the eight chapters:

Eight Shifts to Start Becoming a Future-Ready Church

SHIFT	DATED QUESTION	BETTER QUESTION
From attendance to attachment: making sure **"membership"** includes identity-shaping **relationships**	How are we growing church membership and attendance?	How can we help more people develop healthy spiritual relationships in their complex lives?
From nuclear families to forged families: expanding beyond a **particular family ideal** to **building community** for people in various stages of life	How can we get more people to volunteer so that we can strengthen ministry to the families in our church?	How can our church's family ministries build health and increased capacity in people so that they can be more available to those who are lonely, struggling, or feeling that they don't fit in?
From mind to soul: broadening our message to include an **apologetic of empathy**	How do we convince unchurched friends to develop more interest in eternal things?	How can we enter more people's pain and show them the God who cares?
From church refugees to church as refuge: moving from happenstance **homogeneity** to unification through **hospitality**	How can we stay a "big happy family" by reaching more people like us?	How can a culture of irresistible hospitality unify our congregation's increasing diversity?
From silence to righteousness: taking risks to apply the implications of the gospel that speak to **justice**	Should our weekend sermon or pulpit prayers specifically mention the justice issue that's been so much in the news this week?	Where does our church need to become more specific in applying a grander and more transcendent vision for biblical justice?
From racial tension to community blessing: moving beyond **tokenism** to genuine **diversity**	How can we help minorities feel more included in our church?	How can our church push the boundaries of what it means to be ethnically inclusive and diverse?
From physical only to healthy hybrid: expanding **in-person meetings** to develop seamless transitions into **digital discipleship**	How do we do in-person church better so that people will want to spend less time online?	How can we discern God's work everywhere people spend time, especially in the growing digital world?
From numbers to vitality: seeking church health by improving on **one model** of church to embrace **multiple modes** of church	How are we doing in terms of attendance, budget, and facilities?	How is God at work through various modes of church, and how can we become more aligned with healthy ways to grow the church?

Zondervan grants permission for fee-free reprints of this page from *Becoming a Future-Ready Church* by Daniel Yang, Adelle Banks, and Warren Bird. ©2024.

Will the Next Generation Run
with What It Inherits?

To bluntly ask the biggest question behind this book: Will the young people in your church, when given the reins at the proper time, want and be able to lead what you're passing on to them?

"This is what they'll inherit, so they have no choice," you might respond. Or do they?

Each new generation will inherit not only our faith and its biblical foundations but also all kinds of cultural artifacts like pulpits and microphones, tax-exemption requirements, traditions, systems, community reputations, and much more. How well will the trappings and structures you hand to the next generation help it to lead for the future? In training future leaders, will you allow and encourage them to not just fill your shoes but create new shoes as needed? Will you allow and encourage them to not just fill your seats but create new chairs—and tables—as needed? These are very real issues, going far beyond physical architecture, where smaller seats with hat holders underneath in churches of the 1800s have become bigger seats with both padding and cupholders in the 2000s.

The next generation will be navigating the same unchanging mission from Jesus, but they'll be doing it within a different environment. That's why you need to create space for tomorrow's leaders to emerge, develop, be empowered, and take appropriate ownership for the future. Listening and learning must take place among all parties involved—both mentoring *and* reverse mentoring must happen. The generations currently "in charge" can't move forward well unless rising generations are at the table, perhaps even meeting at places of **Younger generations need to be speaking and not just listening.** *their* choice rather than inside the walls of the church. Younger generations need to be speaking and not just listening. That's how you can keep your leadership pathway agile and enduring.

Keep Your Church's Leadership Pathway from Being Curtailed

This book has implied a dual imperative for churches: stay alive and flourish today while at the same time build and retool for tomorrow. Therefore, the success of this book will be measured by how well it engages young leaders in conversations about tomorrow's church that's yet to emerge. In that arena, we want to make innovators and future innovators the heroes at your church.

Chapter 1 referenced the moment in 1 Samuel 17 when David offered to fight Goliath. Does "Saul's armor" prevent your church from preparing for 2050? Saul had offered to give David his best-known strategy, technology, and equipment: his own armor, which had worked so well for him. David tried it on but decided that he couldn't succeed with it, so he offered an alternative—not only his total dependence on God (vv. 37, 45–47) but also methods he knew and had already tested (vv. 39–40).

Put yourself in the mind of Saul and his advisers at that moment, and compare your response to how you view your church today. Which of these options best fits you?

- Do you agree that a problem exists—that too much of today's "armor" will be inadequate for tomorrow's challenges?
- Do you see the problem, but not know what to change?
- Do you see the problem and agree that changes need to happen, but don't feel ready?
- Do you see the problem and agree that changes need to happen, but don't know how?
- Do you see yourself among those intentionally making changes and making room so young leaders feel excited and confident for the future?

We recommend that the best pathway forward will come from prayer-filled healthy leadership discussions with multiple people,

Figure 10.2—Sharp Increase in the "Nones"

Generation	Nones	Atheist/Agnostic	Protestant	Catholic	Other World Religions
Silent (born 1925-1945)	12%	7%	51%	24%	6%
Boomers (born 1946-1964)	18%	9%	46%	21%	6%
Gen X (born 1965-1976)	26%	13%	37%	19%	5%
Millennials (born 1977-1995)	30%	17%	28%	17%	8%
Gen Z (born 1996-2019)	34%	17%	23%	16%	10%

Cooperative Election Study, 2020–2022, analyzed by Ryan Burge; image courtesy ECFA.

including those from the rising generations, just as Saul was willing to give over a pivotal leadership moment to young David. In fact, whatever Saul's actual motives were,[3] he went on to fully bless his future successor with the words, "Go, and the LORD be with you!" (v. 37).

Remember Maurice and Elizabeth

Let's conclude by talking about your neighbors and ours. A painful number of them are "never attenders" of church. Across this book we've described many types of churches that are trying to reach them, from house churches to megachurches and from online communities to hybrid and in-person congregations.

A somewhat parallel group are those who identify as "nones," telling survey takers—as Maurice did in chapter 2—that they have no religious preference. Our nation's current trajectory forecasts that the fastest-growing segment of the population will be people like Maurice and his sister Elizabeth, both in the "nothing in particular" category. Figure 10.2 affirms that a growing number of Maurices and Elizabeths live in your community and ours. The data[4] is clear that much larger percentages of younger generations enter adulthood with no religious affiliation than ever before. In fact, the share of people moving into adulthood without a religious attachment has tripled in the past thirty years. To rephrase, roughly one in three Americans coming of age today were raised with no religious affiliation.

Roughly one in three Americans coming of age today were raised with no religious affiliation.

If you believe that Maurice, Elizabeth, and their many friends are very reachable (as we do), then which of the "from this to that" shifts in this book will be your starting point for conversation within your church? As you develop appropriate pathways to help Maurices and Elizabeths find a sense of belonging inside your church and serve the community around it, then your congregation will be on the right track to prepare disciple-making disciples of Jesus Christ for 2050.

Too many church narratives are about decline or disillusion. We've wanted to provide church leaders—both paid and volunteer—with a thoughtful and hopeful trajectory for the future. We've wanted to stoke your imagination so you can see that God's church not only has great chapters ahead but is also a part of creating a better society for the future. This vision requires today's church leaders to think about how they are setting up the next generation—and working in healthy partnership with it.

We want to see church leaders move from handwringing to hope.

We want to see church leaders move from handwringing to hope. And we want each of your conversations to remind you that the future is already now.

Notes

Foreword

1. Ryan P. Burge, *The Nones: Where They Came From, Who They Are, and Where They Are Going*, 2nd ed. (Minneapolis: Fortress, 2023); data from the General Social Survey, 1972–2022.
2. Ryan Burge, "The Nones Have Hit a Ceiling," *Graphs about Religion*, May 20, 2024, https://www.graphsaboutreligion.com/p/the-nones -have-hit-a-ceiling/; data from the Cooperative Election Study, 2008–2023.
3. Jim Davis and Michael Graham, *The Great Dechurching: Who's Leaving, Why Are They Going, and What Will It Take to Bring Them Back?* (Grand Rapids: Zondervan, 2023); data from the Cooperative Election Study, 2008–2023; and the United States Census Bureau.
4. Ryan Burge, "The Aftermath of the Schism in the United Methodist Church," *Graphs about Religion*, April 25, 2024, https://www .graphsaboutreligion.com/p/the-aftermath-of-the-schism-in-the/; data from the United Methodist Church's own denominational records.
5. Ryan Burge, "The State of the Southern Baptist Convention in 2023," *Graphs about Religion*, May 8, 2024, https://www.graphsaboutreligion .com/p/the-state-of-the-southern-baptist/; data from the SBC's denominational records compiled and disseminated by Lifeway Research.
6. Ryan Burge, "Just How Bad Is Denominational Decline?," *Graphs about Religion*, June 12, 2023, https://www.graphsaboutreligion.com/p/just

-how-bad-is-denominational-decline/; data from each denomination's membership records.

7. Ryan Burge, "The Future of American Christianity Is Non-Denominational," *Graphs about Religion*, July 24, 2023, https://www .graphsaboutreligion.com/p/the-future-of-american-christianity/; data from the General Social Survey, 1972–2022.

8. Burge, "Just How Bad Is Denominational Decline?"; data from each denomination's membership records.

9. Ryan Burge, "Americans Still Overwhelmingly Believe in God," *Graphs about Religion*, May 25, 2023, https://www.graphsaboutreligion.com /p/americans-still-overwhelmingly-believe/; data from the General Social Survey, 1988–2022.

10. Burge, "The Nones Have Hit a Ceiling"; data from the Cooperative Election Study, 2008–2023.

Preface

1. See William Vanderbloemen and Warren Bird, *Next: Pastoral Succession That Works*, rev. ed. (Grand Rapids: Baker, 2020).

Chapter 1: Why We Need Future-Ready Churches

1. Elmer Towns, *The Ten Largest Sunday Schools and What Makes Them Grow* (Grand Rapids: Baker, 1969).

2. Doug Livingston, "Megachurch Back on Market," *Akron Beacon Journal*, June 10, 2019, https://www.beaconjournal.com/story/lifestyle /faith/2019/06/10/megachurch-back-on-market/4835210007/.

3. Jennifer Conn, "Once-Segregated Akron Baptist Temple Sold to The Word Church," Cleveland, May 21, 2018, https://www.cleveland.com /akron/2018/05/formerly_segregated_akron_bapt.html/.

4. Colette Jenkins, "Akron Baptist Temple Selling Its Building and Planning to Relocate," *Akron Beacon Journal*, August 9, 2015, https:// www.beaconjournal.com/story/lifestyle/faith/2015/08/09/akron -baptist-temple-selling-its/10724470007/.

5. Livingston, "Megachurch Back on Market."

6. Doug Livingston, "Once among Biggest U.S. Churches, Empty Akron Baptist Temple Now Home to Looters, Squatters," *Akron*

Beacon Journal, November 18, 2021, https://www.beaconjournal
.com/story/news/2021/11/18/akron-baptist-temple-kenmore-could
-get-demolished-redevelopment/6234281001/. See also Ruin Road,
"Abandoned Mega Church: Akron Baptist Temple," YouTube video,
April 6, 2024, https://www.youtube.com/watch?v=OwF8iOSghOI&ab
_channel=RuinRoad/.

7. Derek Kreider, "Demolition Begins at The Word Church in Akron,
One of the Country's First Megachurches," *Akron Beacon Journal*,
March 19, 2024, https://www.beaconjournal.com/story/news/local
/2024/03/19/demolition-of-the-former-akron-baptist-temple-begins
/72993120007/.

8. Robert D. Putnam and David E. Campbell, *American Grace: How Religion
Divides and Unites Us* (New York: Simon and Schuster, 2012), 83.

9. George Gallup and D. Michael Lindsay, *Surveying the Religious
Landscape Trends in U.S. Beliefs* (Harrisburg, PA: Morehouse, 1999),
7, 19. See also Robert Wuthnow, *After the Baby Boomers: How Twenty-
and Thirty-Somethings Are Shaping the Future of American Religion*
(Princeton: Princeton University Press, 2007), 80.

10. Frank Newport, "Majority Still Says Religion Can Answer Today's
Problems," Gallup, June 27, 2014, https://news.gallup.com/poll/171998
/majority-says-religion-answer-today-problems.aspx/.

11. Eileen Lindner, "Church Property in a Diminishing Religious
Footprint," in *Gone for Good?: Negotiating the Coming Wave of Church
Property Transition*, ed. Mark Elsdon (Grand Rapids: Eerdmans, 2024),
24. See also Putnam and Campbell, *American Grace*, 82–87.

12. Robert S. Ellwood, *The Fifties Spiritual Marketplace: American Religion
in a Decade of Conflict* (New Brunswick, NJ: Rutgers University Press,
1997), 1.

13. Tim Keller, "The Decline and Renewal of the American Church," 2022,
https://rpc-download.s3.amazonaws.com/Quarterly-Tim_Keller
-Decline_and_Renewal_of_the_American_Church-Extended
.pdf?button/, 4.

14. These are all part of some three thousand Christ-centered ministries
and churches currently accredited by the Evangelical Council for
Financial Accountability (ECFA).

15. Ryan Burge, "Four of the Most Dramatic Shifts in American Religion Over the Last 50 Years," July 10, 2023, https://www .graphsaboutreligion.com/p/four-of-the-most-dramatic-shifts/. See also https://www.graphsaboutreligion.com/p/just-how-bad-is -denominational-decline/.

16. Dean Kelley, *Why Conservative Churches Are Growing: A Study in Sociology of Religion* (Macon, GA: Mercer University Press, 1996), 1.

17. Paul Saffo, "Six Rules for Effective Forecasting," *Harvard Business Review* (July–August, 2007), https://hbr.org/2007/07/six-rules-for -effective-forecasting/.

18. Nate Cohn, "Big Drop in Share of Americans Calling Themselves Christian," *The New York Times*, May 12, 2015, https://www.nytimes .com/2015/05/12/upshot/big-drop-in-share-of-americans-calling -themselves-christian.html?searchResultPosition=1/.

19. Jim Davis and Michael Graham, *The Great Dechurching: Who's Leaving, Why Are They Going, and What Will It Take to Get Them Back?* (Grand Rapids: Zondervan, 2023), 62, 120.

20. Jeffery Fulks, Randy Petersen, and John Farquhar Plake, "State of the Bible: USA 2023," American Bible Society, https://1s712.americanbible .org/state-of-the-bible/stateofthebible/State_of_the_bible-2023.pdf, 21.

21. Warren Bird and Jake Lapp, *ECFA 2023 State of Giving*, 14th ed. (ECFA, 2023), 14, https://www.ecfa.org/stateofgiving/pdf/SOG_2023_FINAL .pdf. See also "Giving USA: Total U.S. Charitable Giving Declined in 2022 to $499.33 Billion Following Two Years of Record Generosity," Indiana University Indianapolis, June 20, 2023, https://philanthropy .indianapolis.iu.edu/news-events/news/_news/2023/giving-usa-total -us-charitable-giving-declined-in-2022-to-49933-billion-following-two -years-of-record-generosity.html/.

22. Faith Communities Today and Hartford Institute for Religion Research, "Back to Normal? The Mixed Messages of Congregational Recovery Coming Out of the Pandemic," August 2023, https://www .covidreligionresearch.org/wp-content/uploads/2023/09/Epic-4-2.pdf, 2–3.

23. Faith Communities Today and Hartford Institute for Religion Research, 8–11.

24. "2022 CIRP Freshman Survey," Higher Education Research Institute at UCLA (Los Angeles: Regents of the University of California, 2023), https://heri.ucla.edu/wp-content/uploads/2023/10/DATA-TABLES -TFS-2022.pdf.

25. Becka A. Alper, Michael Rotolo, Patricia Tevington, Justin Nortey, and Asta Kallo, "Spirituality among Americans," Pew Research Center, December 7, 2023, https://www.pewresearch.org/religion/2023/12/07 /spirituality-among-americans/.

26. "8 in 10 Americans Say Religion Is Losing Influence in Public Life," Pew Research Center, March 15, 2024, https://www.pewresearch .org/religion/2024/03/15/8-in-10-americans-say-religion-is-losing -influence-in-public-life/.

27. "Attendance at Religious Services," Pew Research Center, accessed July 8, 2024, https://www.pewresearch.org/religion/religious-landscape-study /attendance-at-religious-services#attendance-at-religious-services/.

28. "Religion and Congregations in a Time of Social and Political Upheaval," Figure 18, Public Religion Research Institute, May 16, 2023, https://www.prri.org/research/religion-and-congregations-in-a-time -of-social-and-political-upheaval/.

29. Bob Buford, *Drucker & Me: What a Texas Entrepreneur Learned from the Father of Modern Management* (Franklin, TN: Worthy, 2014), 55.

30. Statistics from Scott W. Sunquist, *The Unexpected Christian Century: The Reversal and Transformation of Global Christianity, 1900–2000* (Grand Rapids: Baker Academic, 2015), 1.

Chapter 2: From Attendance to Attachment

1. Jeffrey M. Jones, "U.S. Church Membership Falls below Majority for First Time," Gallup, March 29, 2021, https://news.gallup.com/poll /341963/church-membership-falls-below-majority-first-time.aspx/.

2. Stephanie Kramer, "Modeling the Future of Religion in America," Pew Research Center, September 13, 2022, https://www.pewresearch .org/religion/wp-content/uploads/sites/7/2022/09/US-Religious -Projections_FOR-PRODUCTION-9.13.22.pdf.

3. Mark Chaves, *American Religion: Contemporary Trends*, 2nd ed. (Princeton: Princeton University Press, 2017), xiii–xiv, 13, 117–18.

4. Zach Hrynowski and Stephanie Marken, "Gen Z Voices Lackluster Trust in Major U.S. Institutions," Gallup, September 14, 2023, https://news.gallup.com/opinion/gallup/510395/gen-voices-lackluster-trust-major-institutions.aspx/.

5. Elizabeth Drescher, *Choosing Our Religion: The Spiritual Lives of America's Nones* (New York: Oxford University Press, 2016).

6. Drescher, *Choosing Our Religion*, 118.

7. Drescher, *Choosing Our Religion*, 155.

8. Ryan P. Burge, *The Nones: Where They Came From, Who They Are, and Where They Are Going*, 2nd ed. (Minneapolis: Fortress, 2023), 204.

9. For more about Life.Church's history, see this article from Life.Church's denomination: https://covchurch.org/2021/01/21/life-church-growth-unimaginable-25-years-ago/.

10. According to a 2015 Pew Research Center study, one in five adults were raised in an interfaith home and 27 percent of millennials came from religiously mixed homes. See "One-in-Five U.S. Adults Were Raised in Interfaith Homes," Pew Research Center, October 26, 2016, https://www.pewresearch.org/religion/2016/10/26/one-in-five-u-s-adults-were-raised-in-interfaith-homes/.

11. "Religious and Spiritual Practice: How Faith Leaders Can Support Gen Z Mental Health," Springtide Research Institute, May 16, 2023, https://www.springtideresearch.org/post/mental-health/religious-and-spiritual-practice-how-faith-leaders-can-support-gen-z-mental-health.

12. For a more in-depth discussion about the human need for belonging, see R. F. Baumeister, "Need-to-Belong Theory" in *Handbook of Theories of Social Psychology*, ed. Paul A. M. Van Lange, Arie W. Kruglanski, and E. Tory Higgins, vol. 2 (Thousand Oaks, CA: Sage, 2011), 121–40, https://doi.org/10.4135/9781446249222.n32/.

Chapter 3: From Nuclear Families to Forged Families

1. The American longing for stability during the World War II era was locked in time with Norman Rockwell's iconic painting *Freedom from Want*, showing a happy family at Thanksgiving dinner, which appeared in the March 6, 1943 edition of *The Saturday Evening Post*.

2. Roberta L. Coles, *Race and Family: A Structural Approach*, 2nd ed. (Lanham, MD: Rowman & Littlefield, 2016), 49–50.

3. *Modern Family*, Television Academy, accessed July 8, 2024, https://www.emmys.com/shows/modern-family/.

4. Jay Pritchett is played by Ed O'Neill, who is just as known, if not more, for playing Al Bundy on the family sitcom *Married . . . with Children* (1987–1997), a sitcom parody about the nuclear family in America.

5. Christy Bieber, "Revealing Divorce Statistics In 2024," *Forbes*, January 8, 2024, https://www.forbes.com/advisor/legal/divorce/divorce-statistics/. While *Forbes* is a business magazine, the statistics in this article are taken from reputable sources such as the Centers for Disease Control and Prevention and the U.S. Census Bureau.

6. Stephanie Kramer, "U.S. Has World's Highest Rate of Children Living in Single-Parent Households," Pew Research Center, December 12, 2019, https://www.pewresearch.org/short-reads/2019/12/12/u-s-children-more-likely-than-children-in-other-countries-to-live-with-just-one-parent/.

7. Brittany Rico, Rose M. Kreider, and Lydia Anderson, "Growth in Interracial and Interethnic Married-Couple Households," U.S. Census Bureau, July 9, 2018, https://www.census.gov/library/stories/2018/07/interracial-marriages.html/.

8. Daniel A. Cox, "Emerging Trends and Enduring Patterns in American Family Life," Survey Center on American Life, February 9, 2022, https://www.americansurveycenter.org/research/emerging-trends-and-enduring-patterns-in-american-family-life/.

9. Bill Chappell, "Supreme Court Declares Same-Sex Marriage Legal in All 50 States," *The Two-Way* (blog), NPR, June 26, 2015, https://www.npr.org/sections/thetwo-way/2015/06/26/417717613/supreme-court-rules-all-states-must-allow-same-sex-marriages/.

10. David Brooks, "David Brooks on Faith in Polarized Times," BioLogos, May 23, 2022, https://biologos.org/resources/david-brooks-on-faith-in-polarized-times/.

11. David Brooks, "The Nuclear Family Was a Mistake," *The Atlantic*, March 2020, https://www.theatlantic.com/magazine/archive/2020/03/the-nuclear-family-was-a-mistake/605536/.

12. Brooks, "The Nuclear Family Was a Mistake."

13. Andrew T. Walker, "The Church as Forged Family: A Reply to David Brooks," *Institute for Family Studies*, February 19, 2020, https:// ifstudies.org/blog/the-church-as-forged-family-a-reply-to-david -brooks/.

14. Robert J. Banks, *Paul's Idea of Community: Spirit and Culture in Early House Churches*, 3rd ed. (Grand Rapids: Baker Academic, 2020), 7.

15. Banks, *Paul's Idea of Community*, 13.

16. Margaret Mowczko, "Lydia of Thyatira: The Founding Member of the Philippian Church," *Marg Mowczko* (blog), November 30, 2017, https:// margmowczko.com/lydia-of-thyatira-philippi/.

17. Ross Douthat, "Waking Up in 2030," *The New York Times*, June 27, 2020, https://www.nytimes.com/2020/06/27/opinion/sunday/us -coronavirus-2030.html/.

18. "Suicide Statistics," American Foundation for Suicide Prevention, May 19, 2023, https://afsp.org/suicide-statistics/.

Chapter 4: From Mind to Soul

1. Jeffrey M. Jones, "Belief in God in U.S. Dips to 81%, a New Low," Gallup, June 17, 2022, https://news.gallup.com/poll/393737/belief-god-dips -new-low.aspx/. See also Stephen Bullivant, *Nonverts: The Making of Ex-Christian America* (New York: Oxford University Press), 2022.

2. According to the U.S. Census Bureau, in 2020 there were 258.3 million adults, 78 percent of the total population. We calculated the 50 million number using the U.S. population growth projected by Statista for 2024, which is 336.6 million total population or 262.5 million adults. See "Total Population of the United States from 2015 to 2027," Statista, April 2023, https://www.statista.com/statistics /263762/total-population-of-the-united-states/. The adult population continues to increase at a faster rate than the general population; see Stella U. Ogunwole, Megan A. Rabe, Andrew W. Roberts, and Zoe Caplan, "Population under Age 18 Declined Last Decade," U.S. Census Bureau, August 12, 2021, https://www.census.gov/library/stories/2021 /08/united-states-adult-population-grew-faster-than-nations-total -population-from-2010-to-2020.html.

3. George M. Marsden, *Religion and American Culture: A Brief History*, 3rd ed. (Grand Rapids: Eerdmans, 2018), 386 (emphasis added).

4. Ed Stetzer, "Why Rachel Held Evans Mattered," *Outreach*, May 6, 2019, https://outreachmagazine.com/features/discipleship/42703-why -rachel-held-evans-mattered.html/.

5. Rachel Held Evans, *Searching for Sunday: Loving, Leaving, and Finding the Church* (Nashville: Thomas Nelson, 2015), 75.

6. Rachel Held Evans and Jeff Chu, *Wholehearted Faith* (New York: HarperOne, 2022), 113.

7. Abby Ohlheiser, "The Woman behind 'Me Too' Knew the Power of the Phrase When She Created It—10 Years Ago," *Washington Post*, October 19, 2017, https://www.washingtonpost.com/news/the-- intersect/wp/2017/10/19/the-woman-behind-me-too-knew-the-power -of-the-phrase-when-she-created-it-10-years-ago/.

8. Blake Chastain, "Blake Chastain," *Blake Chastain*, accessed July 8, 2024, https://blakechastain.com/.

9. Ruth Tsuria, "Get Out of Church! The Case of #EmptyThePews: Twitter Hashtag between Resistance and Community," *Information* 11, no. 6 (June 2020): 335, https://doi.org/10.3390/info11060335/.

10. See the Vancouver section in "2021 Census of Population," Statistics Canada, November 15, 2023, https://www12.statcan.gc.ca/census -recensement/2021/dp-pd/prof/details/page.cfm?Lang=E&SearchText =vancouver&DGUIDlist=2021A00055915020,2021S05100973 ,2021A00055915022&GENDERlist=1&STATISTIClist=1&HEADERlist=0.

11. "Our Founder," Jude 3 Project, accessed July 8, 2024, https:// jude3project.org/our-founder/.

12. Diane Langberg, *Suffering and the Heart of God: How Trauma Destroys and Christ Restores* (Greensboro, NC: New Growth Press, 2015), 10 (emphasis original).

13. "Moralistic therapeutic deism" is a phrase coined by sociologist Christian Smith in his 2005 book *Soul Searching: The Religious and Spiritual Lives of American Teenagers*, based on the National Study of Youth and Religion, a large-scale project funded by the Lilly Endowment which aimed to explore the religious and spiritual beliefs, practices, and experiences of American teenagers.

14. Adapted from the lecture "Framing Interreligious Dialogue in Evangelical Mission," given by Daniel Yang at the Evangelical Theological Society National Conference on October 9, 2020.

Chapter 5: From Church Refugees to Church as Refuge

1. See Carl S. Dudley, Theresa Zingery, and David Breeden, "Insights into Congregation Conflict," Faith Communities Today, 2019, https://faithcommunitiestoday.org/wp-content/uploads/2019/01/Insights -Into-Congregational-Conflict.pdf.

2. For a more in-depth conversation on church refugees in America, see Josh Packard and Ashleigh Hope, *Church Refugees: Sociologists Reveal Why People Are DONE with Church but Not Their Faith* (Loveland, CO: Group, 2015).

3. Bill Bishop with Robert G. Cushing, *The Big Sort: Why the Clustering of Like-Minded America Is Tearing Us Apart* (Boston: Mariner Books, 2009), 199.

4. Bishop and Cushing, *The Big Sort*, 173.

5. Ed Stetzer, "3 Trends Shaping the Post-Pandemic Church," *Outreach*, September 3, 2021, https://outreachmagazine.com/features/leadership /68856-3-trends-shaping-the-post-pandemic-church.html/.

6. Aaron Earls, "Evangelicals Back Immigration Reform, Increased Border Security," Lifeway Research, February 28, 2024, https://research.lifeway.com/2024/02/28/evangelicals-back-immigration -reform-increased-border-security/.

7. Eugene Scott, "Billy Graham's Son: We Should Halt All Immigration," CNN, December 15, 2015, https://www.cnn.com/2015/12/15/politics /franklin-graham-halt-all-immigration/index.html/.

8. For an array on the history of America and xenophobia, see Erika Lee, *America for Americans: A History of Xenophobia in the United States* (New York: Basic, 2019) and Kevin Kruse and Julian E. Zelizer, eds., *Myth America: Historians Take On the Biggest Legends and Lies about Our Past* (New York: Basic, 2022).

9. Afe Adogame, Raimundo C. Barreto, and Wanderley Pereira da Rosa, eds., *Migration and Public Discourse in World Christianity*, World Christianity and Public Religion 2 (Minneapolis: Fortress, 2019), 233.

10. Rodney Stark, *The Rise of Christianity: How the Obscure, Marginal Jesus Movement Became the Dominant Religious Force in the Western World in a Few Centuries* (San Francisco: HarperSanFrancisco, 1997), 197.

11. Stark, *The Rise of Christianity*, 203.

12. We realize that the topic of leading and preaching amid intense cultural polarization is worthy of addressing at a very practical level. Adelle Banks has written on this in her article "Preaching to Polarized Congregations: A Responsibility and a Challenge, Clergy Say," Religion News Service, December 8, 2023, https://religionnews.com/2023/12/08/preaching-to-polarized-congregations-a-responsibility-and-a-challenge-clergy-say/. For another resource, see Matthew D. Kim and Paul A. Hoffman, *Preaching to a Divided Nation: A Seven-Step Model for Promoting Reconciliation and Unity* (Grand Rapids: Baker Academic, 2022).

13. Christine D. Pohl, *Making Room: Recovering Hospitality as a Christian Tradition* (Grand Rapids: Eerdmans, 1999), 97.

14. Andy Stanley, "Creating a Church of Grace and Truth," *Outreach Magazine*, September 24, 2012, https://outreachmagazine.com/features/4897-becoming-a-church-of-grace-and-truth.html.

Chapter 6: From Silence to Righteousness

1. John Della Volpe, *Fight: How Gen Z Is Channeling Their Fear and Passion to Save America* (New York: St. Martin's Press, 2022), 13–14.

2. "Generation Z Social Issues & Their Impact On Society," United Way NCA, December 1, 2022, https://unitedwaynca.org/blog/gen-Z-social-issues/.

3. Becka A. Alper, "How Religion Intersects with Americans' Views on the Environment," Pew Research Center, November 17, 2022, https://www.pewresearch.org/religion/2022/11/17/how-religion-intersects-with-americans-views-on-the-environment/.

4. See Virgilio Viana, "Health Climate Justice and Deforestation in the Amazon," in *Health of People, Health of Planet and Our Responsibility: Climate Change, Air Pollution and Health*, ed. Wael K. Al-Delaimy, Veerabhadran Ramanathan, and Marcelo Sánchez Sorondo (Cham,

Switzerland: Springer International, 2020), 165–74, https://doi.org/10.1007/978-3-030-31125-4_13.

5. For how some Christians have advocated for climate justice, see Lausanne Movement's Creation Care network (https://lausanne.org/networks/issues/creation-care) or "A Faithful Voice on Hunger and Climate Justice," Bread for the World, October 31, 2022, https://www.bread.org/article/a-faithful-voice-on-hunger-and-climate-justice/.

6. Karen Swallow Prior, *The Evangelical Imagination: How Stories, Images, and Metaphors Created a Culture in Crisis* (Grand Rapids: Brazos, 2023), 3.

7. Jemar Tisby, *How to Fight Racism: Courageous Christianity and the Journey toward Racial Justice* (Grand Rapids: Zondervan, 2023), 63–81.

8. Susie Gamez, "What's in a Name (Wk. 1) El Roi—Susie Gamez—Live Stream Service Rebroadcast," Midtown Church Sacramento, June 4, 2023, YouTube video, 1:16:01, https://www.youtube.com/watch?v=CbLU-eZmqAI/.

9. "Amy Sherman," Sagamore Institute, accessed July 8, 2024, https://sagamoreinstitute.org/bio-amy-sherman/.

10. Jorge Rodriguez, "SO PROUD of the Way the Folks at Grace," Facebook, May 6, 2023, https://www.facebook.com/jorgebelkis/posts/pfbid0eGDqQSiJHrasiBqAiyB65aLUf1onmWpAS8T4zyl1boiTGATErFcMnv9AdCed5De4l/.

Chapter 7: From Racial Tension to Community Blessing

1. Kevin D. Dougherty, Mark Chaves, and Michael O. Emerson, "Racial Diversity in U.S. Congregations, 1998–2019," *Journal for the Scientific Study of Religion* 59, no. 4 (2020): 651–62, https://doi.org/10.1111/jssr.12681.

2. Korie Little Edwards, *The Elusive Dream: The Power of Race in Interracial Churches*, updated ed. (New York: Oxford University Press, 2021).

3. Korie Little Edwards, "The Multiethnic Church Movement Hasn't Lived Up to Its Promise," *Christianity Today*, February 16, 2021, https://www.christianitytoday.com/ct/2021/march/race-diversity-multiethnic-church-movement-promise.html/.

4. William H. Frey, "The Nation Is Diversifying Even Faster Than Predicted, According to New Census Data," Brookings Institution, July 1, 2020, https://www.brookings.edu/articles/new-census-data -shows-the-nation-is-diversifying-even-faster-than-predicted/.

5. William H. Frey, "New 2020 Census Results Show Increased Diversity Countering Decade-Long Declines in America's White and Youth Populations," Brookings Institution, August 13, 2021, https://www .brookings.edu/articles/new-2020-census-results-show-increased -diversity-countering-decade-long-declines-in-americas-white-and -youth-populations/.

6. William H. Frey, "The US Will Become 'Minority White' in 2045, Census Projects," Brookings Institution, March 14, 2018, https://www .brookings.edu/articles/the-us-will-become-minority-white-in-2045 -census-projects/.

7. Scholars have suggested that the early growth of Abraham's people, which started out as a single family, in part came through other people joining the Hebrews during their bondage in Egypt and the amalgamation of other nations into Israel as it contended for the land of Canaan.

8. "Historical Estimates of World Population," U.S. Census Bureau, December 5, 2022, https://www.census.gov/data/tables/time-series /demo/international-programs/historical-est-worldpop.html/.

9. Jessica M. Barron and Rhys H. Williams, *The Urban Church Imagined: Religion, Race, and Authenticity in the City* (New York: NYU Press, 2017), 20.

10. Barron and Williams, *The Urban Church Imagined*, 94–95.

11. This list was generated based on information gathered through the following sources:

   - "Tokenism," IResearchNet, October 6, 2016, https://psychology .iresearchnet.com/counseling-psychology/multicultural-- counseling/tokenism/.
   - Andy Crouch, *Strong and Weak: Embracing a Life of Love, Risk and True Flourishing* (Downers Grove: IVP, 2016).

12. The Southern Poverty Law Center describes Kinism as a racist

interpretation of Christian theology, deriving its name from a phrase for one's blood relatives. Kinism "refers to the belief that biblical scripture specifically proscribes interracial marriage, integration and racial equality, and promotes white nationalism." See Hatewatch Staff, "Racist Website Faith and Heritage Is Closing Up Shop," The Southern Poverty Law Center, January 29, 2019, https://www.splcenter.org/hatewatch /2019/01/29/racist-website-faith-and-heritage-closing-shop/.

13. Mark DeYmaz, "Ethnic Blends: Growing Healthy, Multiethnic Churches," Lifeway Research, October 9, 2014, https://research .lifeway.com/2014/10/09/ethnic-blends-growing-healthy-multiethnic -churches/.

14. Denise Kimber Buell, *Why This New Race: Ethnic Reasoning in Early Christianity* (New York: Columbia University Press, 2005), 139.

15. Henry A. Buchanan and Bob W. Brown, "Integration: Great Dilemma of the Church: Nation's Foremost Moral Issue Forces Reappraisal of Racially Separate Worship," *Ebony* magazine, June 1966, 171 (emphasis original).

Chapter 8: From Physical Only to Healthy Hybrid

1. "Home," Roblox, accessed July 8, 2024, https://corp.roblox.com/ (emphasis added).

2. Hristina Nikolovska, "Riveting Roblox Statistics & Facts for 2023," Bankless Times, February 16, 2023, https://www.banklesstimes.com /roblox-statistics/.

3. See, for instance, what Life.Church is doing in the metaverse (https:// www.life.church/metaverse) or how VR Church is accommodating people through VR technology (https://www.vrchurch.org).

4. In 1950, only a third of the world lived in urban areas. Currently, 55 percent of the world's population lives in urban areas while 66 percent have access to the internet and 61 percent are social media users. See "68% of the World Population Projected to Live in Urban Areas by 2050, Says UN," United Nations, May 16, 2018, https://www .un.org/development/desa/en/news/population/2018-revision-of -world-urbanization-prospects.html/ and "Number of Internet and Social Media Users Worldwide as of April 2024," Statista, May 22,

2024, https://www.statista.com/statistics/617136/digital-population
-worldwide/.

5. Heidi A. Campbell and Stephen Garner, *Networked Theology: Negotiating Faith in Digital Culture* (Grand Rapids: Baker Academic, 2016), 36–37.

6. Bryce Ashlin-Mayo, *Digital Mission: A Practical Guide to Ministry Online* (Toronto: Tyndale Academic, 2020), introduction.

7. Mark Zuckerberg, "A Privacy-Focused Vision for Social Networking," Facebook, March 12, 2021, https://www.facebook.com/notes /2420600258234172/.

8. Brian X. Chen, "The Future of Social Media Is a Lot Less Social," *The New York Times*, April 19, 2023, https://www.nytimes.com/2023/04/19 /technology/personaltech/tiktok-twitter-facebook-social.html/.

9. Amy Roeder, "Social Media Use Can Be Positive for Mental Health and Well-Being," Harvard T. H. Chan School of Public Health, January 6, 2020, https://www.hsph.harvard.edu/news/features/social-media -positive-mental-health/. For the entire study, see Mesfin A. Bekalu, Rachel F. McCloud, and K. Viswanath, "Association of Social Media Use With Social Well-Being, Positive Mental Health, and Self-Rated Health: Disentangling Routine Use from Emotional Connection to Use," *Health Education & Behavior* 46, no. 2_suppl. (November 19, 2019): 69S–80S, https://doi.org/10.1177/1090198119863768.

10. Mayank Gupta and Aditya Sharma, "Fear of Missing Out: A Brief Overview of Origin, Theoretical Underpinnings and Relationship with Mental Health," *World Journal of Clinical Cases* 9, no. 19 (July 6, 2021): 4881–89, https://doi.org/10.12998/wjcc.v9.i19.4881/.

11. We conducted a search in ProQuest, a database for scholarly and published academic content, for dissertations in the English language related to "fear of missing out," yielding this number.

12. Fazale R. Rana is a former scientist and Christian apologist who cowrote *Humans 2.0: Scientific, Philosophical, and Theological Perspectives on Transhumanism* (Covina, CA: Reasons to Believe, 2019) and offers reasons for why Christians should partner with technological advancement to share the gospel and to create a higher quality of life, especially among those with the greatest needs in the world. Although the discourse of Rana's book is much broader than

digital ministry, a lot of the concepts he discusses regarding the ethics and practicality of technology in partnership with the gospel can apply to digital ministry.

13. René Ostberg, "Transhumanism," Encyclopedia Britannica, February 2, 2024, https://www.britannica.com/topic/transhumanism/. For a more in-depth conversation on transhumanism from a distinctly Christian perspective, listen to theologian and author Richard Mouw and scholar and inventor Rosalind Picard discuss how to think wisely about transhumanism: https://biologos.org/events/online-understanding -transhumanism/.

14. "Engiven," accessed July 8, 2024, https://www.engiven.com/.

15. James Lawrence, "The Church's Crypto Future, as Told by Engiven's CEO," Pushpay, November 8, 2023, https://pushpay.com/blog/the -churchs-crypto-future/.

16. The Evangelical Council for Financial Accountability (ECFA) regularly offers webinars on how to set up cryptocurrency donations, safeguards for use of cryptocurrency in ministry, and the like. See https://www.ecfa.org/WebinarRecordings.aspx/.

17. "AI and the Church Survey Results," Gloo, accessed July 8, 2024, https://www.gloo.us/ai-survey-results/.

18. As authors, we acknowledge that, along with the whole of society, the church is still very much in the innovation and trial and error stage of how to practically utilize AI. The app "Text with Jesus," created by Catloaf Software, is an example of how some are trying to use AI to help people engage the Bible and biblical characters. See Fiona André, "New AI App Lets Users 'Text with' Jesus and Other Biblical Figures," August 7, 2023, Religion News Service, https://religionnews.com/2023/08/07/new -ai-app-lets-users-text-with-jesus-and-other-biblical-figures/.

19. Jason Thacker, *The Age of AI: Artificial Intelligence and the Future of Humanity* (Grand Rapids: Zondervan, 2020), 181.

20. In his book *Faith in the Age of AI: Christianity through the Looking Glass* (Eleison Press, 2023), Nashville pastor Dan Scott does not specifically delve into the ethics and tactics of AI in the church. However, he provides a framework and metaphors for how to engage a world that is inevitably being shaped by AI.

21. Michelle Faverio, Justin Nortey, Jeff Diamant, and Gregory A. Smith, "Online Religious Services Appeal to Many Americans, but Going in Person Remains More Popular," Pew Research Center, June 2, 2023, https://www.pewresearch.org/religion/2023/06/02/online-religious -services-appeal-to-many-americans-but-going-in-person-remains -more-popular/.

22. Ed Stetzer, Andrew MacDonald, and Enoch Hill, "COVID 19 Church Survey One Year Report," accessed July 8, 2024, https://exponential.org /product/covid-19-church-survey-one-year-report/.

23. Alan Hirsch, *The Forgotten Ways: Reactivating Apostolic Movements*, 2nd ed. (Grand Rapids: Brazos, 2016), 163–64 (emphasis original).

24. The vision of VR MMO Church is "to cultivate loving spiritual communities across the metaverse." VR MMO Church, "Home," accessed July 8, 2024, https://www.vrchurch.org/.

25. The mission of GodSquad Church is to connect online video gamers to God by "meeting them where they are"—that is, in virtual spaces, largely on Twitch. GodSquad Church, "Home," accessed July 8, 2024, https://www.godsquadchurch.com/our-values/.

26. Meta, "Home," accessed July 8, 2024, https://about.meta.com/.

27. Meta, "Company Info," accessed July 8, 2024, https://about.meta.com /company-info/.

28. Sherwood Eliot Wirt, "C. S. Lewis on Heaven, Earth and Outer Space," The Christian Broadcasting Network, n.d., accessed July 8, 2024, https://www.cbn.com/special/Narnia/articles/ans _LewisLastInterviewB.aspx/.

Chapter 9: From Numbers to Vitality

1. Wen Reagan, "Church Growth Movement—Timeline Movement," The Association of Religion Data Archives, accessed July 8, 2024, https://www.thearda.com/us-religion/history/timelines /entry?etype=3&eid=8/.

2. Gary L. McIntosh and Paul Engle, eds., *Evaluating the Church Growth Movement: Five Views* (Grand Rapids: Zondervan, 2010), 23–25. See also Gary L. McIntosh, *Donald A. McGavran: A Biography of the Twentieth Century's Premier Missiologist* (Boca Raton, FL: Church Leadership

Insights, 2015) and Carl George and Warren Bird, *How to Break Growth Barriers: Revise Your Role, Release Your People, and Capture Overlooked Opportunities for Your Church*, rev. ed. (Grand Rapids: Baker, 2017).

3. Admittedly, the historical development of religious groups as nonprofit entities of modern democratic governments—although relevant to the discussion in this book—is too long and complex to unpack here. Suffice to say, while it is not unbiblical to understand the church as a legal organization, the witness from other parts of the world, particularly where churches lack governmental recognition and freedom, gives us tremendous insight into the paradigm of the New Testament church. Modern churches in the Western world, in particular, have much to learn from the persecuted churches around the world.

4. See ECFA's effort to address this problem by raising the standard of care for ministry leaders, https://ecfa.org/LeadershipStandard.aspx/.

5. Heidi A. Campbell and John Dyer, eds., *Ecclesiology for a Digital Church: Theological Reflections on a New Normal* (London: SCM Press, 2022), 100. See also the 2024 reports from ECFA's research of online discipleship and generosity at www.ecfa.org/surveys/.

6. We are not referring to liberation theology or other liberation movements. We are only saying that generations past have rigidly defined the church for themselves based on their cultural norms and needs. Subsequent generations often inherit these definitions without much evaluation.

7. There are a large number of books written around church hurt and trauma. As they occur, high-profile church scandals seem to heighten awareness for the church at large to address these issues. There is no consensus across the literature around the best way to address church hurt, especially because not all circumstances are the same. We acknowledge that there are different kinds of hurt experienced in the church, and some of these instances need to be addressed and engaged outside of church-centric spaces. When at all possible, we believe the journey of healing for Christians who experience hurt in the church should include an element of receiving love, understanding, and support from other Christians and safe church spaces.

8. Sixteen Ramos, "The 'Snowflake' Generation: What Happens When

Mental Toughness Takes a Backseat," LinkedIn, February 21, 2023, https://www.linkedin.com/pulse/snowflake-generation-what--happens-when-mental-toughness-sixteen-ramos/.

9. Amelia Dunlop and Michael Pankowski, "Hey Bosses: Here's What Gen Z Actually Wants at Work," Deloitte Digital, March 26, 2023, https://www.deloittedigital.com/us/en/blog-list/2023/gen-z-research-report.html/.

10. "The Asbury Outpouring," Asbury University, accessed July 8, 2024, https://www.asbury.edu/outpouring/.

11. The "universal church" refers to Christians of all times and places throughout history. It also entails the future reality of the world, particularly when Jesus returns and heaven and earth are fully reconciled.

12. We recommend grasping some of the concepts outlined in Alnoor Ebrahim's *Measuring Social Change: Performance and Accountability in a Complex World* (Stanford, California: Stanford University Press, 2019). Ebrahim is a leading scholar in helping organizations become better by defining metrics of performance around social change.

13. See list in Carl F. George with Warren Bird, *Prepare Your Church for the Future* (Grand Rapids: Revell, 1991), 129–31.

Conclusion

1. Elmer Towns and Warren Bird, *Into the Future: Turning Today's Church Trends into Tomorrow's Opportunities* (Grand Rapids: Revell, 2000), 13.

2. "Our Epidemic of Loneliness and Isolation: The U.S. Surgeon General's Advisory on the Healing Effects of Social Connection and Community," Office of the U.S. Surgeon General, 2023, https://www.hhs.gov/sites/default/files/surgeon-general-social-connection-advisory.pdf.

3. Jordan K. Monson, "The Shepherd Boy Who Wasn't," *Christianity Today*, June 12, 2023, https://www.christianitytoday.com/ct/2023/july-august/shepherd-boy-david-goliath-other-giant.html/.

4. Ryan P. Burge, *20 Myths about Religion and Politics in America* (Minneapolis: Fortress, 2022), 170–71.

Name Index

Scripture Index

Jude

Revelation

Acknowledgments

This book started with Warren Bird, who is always on the lookout for what's bubbling up in churches—issues on the horizon or just around the next corner that need definition and research. His trend-spotting meter surged when his employer, ECFA (the Evangelical Council for Financial Accountability), sent him to an Exponential conference where he attended Daniel Yang's session on "Shaping Factors for the Church of 2050" and heard him say, "So many church leaders are working hard to maintain a church model shaped by the conditions of the 1950s without realizing that today's cultural moment is so much closer to the realities of 2050."

So Warren and Daniel talked, prayed, and began exploring ideas for a book. They decided that featuring real case studies would make the envisioned book far more practical and helpful, warranting a specialized writer who would focus on creating compelling stories. Warren thus presented the idea to Adelle Banks at an academic conference where Warren was speaking and Adelle was reporting.

The three prayed, talked, and ultimately decided to work together on what became *Becoming a Future-Ready Church*. Each coauthor contributed to every chapter, enabling the book to be something far beyond what any of the authors alone could have created.

We authors, each in some way reluctant to take on a project of this scope, want to express thanks for the many people who encouraged the writing of this book, especially colleagues Joan Connell, Dion and Karima

Haynes, and Bob Smietana; the editorial team at Zondervan, particularly Ryan Pazdur, Kyle Rohane, and Daniel Saxton; and the enthusiastic supporters at Exponential, particularly Carrie Williams, Terri Saliba, and Dave Ferguson.

We give special thanks to Dianne Russell for her tremendous support of Warren, and especially for helping frame the graphics that first appeared on the ECFA's Large Church Trends blog. These graphics, after further design and polishing by Travis Huntsman, are prominently reprinted across this book.

We also extend particular thanks to Ryan Burge, PhD, who pointed us to research behind many of these graphics and coached us in how to present it more clearly.

We want to express our gratitude for the many people who gave us excellent feedback on the outline, early drafts, and other stages. They include (alphabetized): Billy and Tasha Asay, Aaron and Hannah Barnett, Gretchen and Daniel Bennett, Michelle Bird, Nathan and Anna Bird, Kara Bettis Carvalho, Marshall Childs, Matt Engel, David Fletcher, Ryan Hartwig, Jeff Irwin, Kep and Deb James, Len Kageler, Jason Knight, Keri Ladouceur, Deante Lavender, Skipp Machmer, Tommy Martin, Marv Nelson, Rick Richardson, Josh Stewart, Scott Thumma, Jim Tomberlin, Elmer Towns, Dave Travis, and Tafie Webb.

We would also like to thank the many family and friends who suggested directions the book might take and helped with fact-checking. They include Martha E. Banks, Chestly Lunday, and Elizabeth Rios.

Finally, we are especially grateful for three incredibly supportive spouses: Linda Yang, Kelvin Childs, and Michelle Bird.

And, most of all, thanks to the God who knows the future, promises abundant wisdom for navigating the pathway ahead, and assures us in Matthew 16:18 that he will build his church, against which even the gates of hell cannot prevail!

About the Authors

Daniel Yang has helped and influenced church networks and movements across North America as a conference speaker, convener, and mission strategy consultant. He has planted churches and trained church planters in global cities across North America including Detroit, Dallas, Toronto, and Chicago.

Yang now serves as the national director of Churches of Welcome for World Relief. He was previously the director of the Church Multiplication Institute at the Wheaton College Billy Graham Center. Daniel has been a pastor, church planter, engineer, and technology consultant. He earned a BS in Computer Science from the University of Michigan, an MDiv from Southwestern Baptist Theological Seminary, and is now pursuing a PhD in Intercultural Studies at Trinity Evangelical Divinity School. He is also the coauthor of *Inalienable: How Marginalized Kingdom Voices Can Help Save the American Church* (IVP, May 2022).

Daniel and his wife, Linda, have five children and live in Aurora, Illinois, where they are mentoring missional church leaders across the western suburbs of Chicagoland.

Adelle Banks is one of the best-known and most respected religion journalists of today's era. She joined Religion News Service (RNS) in 1995 and is its projects editor and national reporter, covering topics including religion and race, congregational issues, and research on faith and society.

Banks's freelance work includes, over the last decade, dozens of interviews with experts on leadership of congregations, colleges, and universities. Banks was honored in 2024 with the Religion News Association's lifetime achievement award and in 2022 with the Washington Association of Black Journalists's inaugural lifetime achievement award. Banks also spearheaded RNS projects that won Wilbur Awards from the Religion Communicators Council in 2021 and 2014.

Banks has received first-place Associated Church Press awards and was the third-place winner of the 2021 Best In-Depth Newswriting on Religion Award from the American Academy of Religion. A Mount Holyoke College graduate, she has also been the religion reporter for two regional newspapers. Banks is a speaker on religion and journalism at gatherings of faith leaders, students, scholars, and communicators.

Warren Bird is a widely published, nationally known researcher of today's church. He oversaw major surveys that uncovered what became the multisite church movement, new trends in megachurches, breakthroughs in church mergers, and patterns that lead to healthy pastoral succession. He has authored or coauthored thirty-four books, including two that have sold more than 100,000 copies each: *Emotionally Healthy Church* by Pete Scazzero and Warren Bird and *Prepare Your Church for the Future* by Carl George and Warren Bird. Other Zondervan publications include *Hero Maker* by Dave Ferguson and Warren Bird.

Bird pastored churches and taught seminary for many years. He then served as research director for Leadership Network and now serves as senior vice president of research for the Evangelical Council for Financial Accountability (ECFA). Bird is also frequently quoted in the media, both in the religious press and mainstream publications.

Bird graduated from Wheaton College (BA, MA), Alliance Theological Seminary (MDiv), and Fordham University (PhD).